A PRACTICAL GUIDE TO HAPPINESS
IN CHILDREN AND TEENS ON THE AUTISM SPECTRUM

A POSITIVE PSYCHOLOGY APPROACH

Victoria Honeybourne

Jessica Kingsley *Publishers*
London and Philadelphia

First published in 2018
by Jessica Kingsley Publishers
73 Collier Street
London N1 9BE, UK
and
400 Market Street, Suite 400
Philadelphia, PA 19106, USA

www.jkp.com

Library of Congress Cataloging in Publication Data
A CIP catalog record for this book is available from the Library of Congress

British Library Cataloguing in Publication Data
A CIP catalogue record for this book is available from the British Library

ISBN 978 1 78592 347 0
eISBN 978 1 78450 681 0

Printed and bound in the United States

The Appendices include printable resources to be used in the activities,
and they are available to download and print from www.jkp.com/
voucher using the code HONEYBOURNEHAPPINESS.

'I...   ...r working with young people on the autis...   ...e author's positive psychology approach to support is really refre... ...g The book is easy to dip into; knowing how busy many teachers/practitioners are, the "top tips" and "if you only have 5 minutes" sections are of great value.'

– Georgina Roycroft, advisory teacher for autism

'It is great to read a book that focuses on happiness. Victoria Honeybourne has written a book that you can read cover to cover if you have an interest in the field, or as a dip-in resource if you are working with a student and need some ideas fast. I can see this being a valuable tool in schools.'

– Kate Bradley, Head of Autism & Inclusion in an Inner London school and co-author of 101 Inclusive and SEN Maths Lessons

'Positive mental health and wellbeing can be a difficult thing to teach, especially when planning for children and young people with autism. This guide…offers practical, easy-to-implement and creative activities that will definitely help promote positive mental health…a great planning tool to all those working with children and young people on the autism spectrum.'

– Claire Brewer, specialist autism teacher and co-author of 101 Inclusive and SEN Maths Lessons

'What a refreshing book this is! Happiness is what we want for our children more than any other thing and this book is filled with practical ideas and activities to build confidence, self-esteem and resilience. This is a fantastic resource for parents and professionals and I'm sure that it will enrich many lives.'

– Adele Devine, special needs teacher, author and co-founder of the multi-award-winning SEN Assist autism software

of related interest

Is It OK to Ask Questions about Autism?
Abi Rawlins
Foreword by Michael Barton
ISBN 978 1 78592 170 4
eISBN 978 1 78450 439 7

Disruptive, Stubborn, Out of Control?
Why kids get confrontational in the classroom, and what to do about it
Bo Hejlskov Elven
ISBN 978 1 78592 212 1
eISBN 978 1 78450 490 8

A Guide to Mental Health Issues in Girls and Young Women on the Autism Spectrum
Diagnosis, Intervention and Family Support
Dr Judy Eaton
ISBN 978 1 78592 092 9
eISBN 978 1 78450 355 0

Attacking Anxiety
A Step-by-Step Guide to an Engaging Approach to Treating Anxiety and Phobias in Children with Autism and Other Developmental Disabilities
Karen Levine and Naomi Chedd
ISBN 978 1 84905 788 2
eISBN 978 1 78450 044 3

The ASD and Me Picture Book
A Visual Guide to Understanding Challenges and Strengths for Children on the Autism Spectrum
Joel Shaul
ISBN 978 1 78592 723 2
eISBN 978 1 78450 351 2

My Book of Feelings
A Book to Help Children with Attachment Difficulties, Learning or Developmental Disabilities Understand their Emotions
Tracey Ross
Illustrated by Rosy Salaman
ISBN 978 1 78592 192 6
eISBN 978 1 78450 466 3

CONTENTS

Note from the Author   6

Introduction   7

1 If You Only Have Five Minutes...   16

2 Understanding the Autism Spectrum   19

3 Understanding Positive Psychology   40

4 Recognising, Identifying and Using Character Strengths   48

5 Cultivating Positive Emotions   77

6 Positive Coping   134

Glossary   181

References   184

Further Reading and Resources   188

Appendix A: Strengths and Definitions Cards   192

Appendix B: Strengths and Definitions List   197

Appendix C: Happiness Survey   199

Appendix D: Happiness Statements   201

Appendix E: Optimist vs. Pessimist Cards   203

Appendix F: Unhopeful Statements   204

Appendix G: Planning Sheet   205

Appendix H: Overcoming Anxieties   206

Appendix I: Dealing with Setbacks   207

Appendix J: Fixed Mindset or Growth Mindset Cards   208

Appendix K: Values List   211

Index of Activities   212

Index   214

NOTE FROM THE AUTHOR

As a woman on the autism spectrum I know how difficult it can be to feel 'happy'. There are all the difficulties that any individual faces, along with the specific challenges created by being autistic and living in a neurotypical world. I hope that this book helps professionals working with young people on the autism spectrum to identify these challenges and enables them to support these children and teens to increase their happiness and wellbeing levels.

Victoria Honeybourne

INTRODUCTION

ABOUT THIS BOOK

This book is a practical guide for professionals working in a variety of contexts with children and young people on the autism spectrum (including those with Asperger Syndrome). It is a guide to promoting emotional wellbeing and happiness in young people on the autism spectrum by using a positive psychology approach. Positive psychology is the scientific, evidence-based study of the positive elements of human existence, such as strengths, positive emotions, and positive coping mechanisms. A range of activities and strategies is suggested for use in mainstream classrooms, small group work and individual interventions. The activities are designed for children and teens roughly between the ages of 7 and 18. The Appendices are available to download and print from www.jkp.com/ voucher using the code HONEYBOURNEHAPPINESS.

AIMS OF THIS BOOK

The aims of this book are:

- to demonstrate how to use findings from the positive psychology movement with young people on the autism spectrum in order to improve their emotional wellbeing and happiness

- to provide practical strategies and approaches that professionals can implement when working with children and young people on the autism spectrum in a range of contexts.

Children and teens on the autism spectrum can face a range of challenges in everyday life and traditionally support has been focused on supporting individuals to achieve academically, to gain employment and to live independently. Although these elements are undoubtedly important, there is actually little evidence that success in education, employment or being able to live independently brings happiness for individuals (whether on the autism spectrum or not). Improving happiness and wellbeing has often been seen as secondary to achieving academic targets. Research now, however, suggests that we need to view this the other way around – success does not necessarily bring happiness, but happiness does tend to bring success! This book is based on that philosophy – by improving happiness and wellbeing in children and teens on the autism spectrum, we place them in a far better position to be able to overcome difficulties, work towards goals and make more informed decisions. Happiness and wellbeing underpin learning and achievement, rather than coming about as a result of these successes. In this book we consider happiness and wellbeing from an autistic point of view – things that make a neurotypical person happy may not be those that make an autistic individual happy, and vice versa! We explore factors that can contribute to happiness, and unhappiness in children and teens on the autism spectrum.

No single resource or activity can act as a 'magic wand' to change young people's emotional wellbeing and happiness levels overnight! The activities and strategies outlined in this book are not intended to be one-off tasks or 'quick fixes', but rather to be ongoing strategies which can be developed and extended over time to meet individual needs and circumstances. The activities in this book aim to gradually equip children and young people with self-knowledge, self-help strategies and a positive attitude, while also gradually changing negative internal dialogues to more positive self-talk. Over time, these small changes, along with changes in how adults working with young people on the autism spectrum communicate, can have a very positive effect on the individual's attitude, outlook and mindset.

REMEMBER! The activities and tasks in this book are designed to increase feelings of happiness and self-esteem; they are intended as preventative measures and not as a substitute for professional mental health input. Children and young people with acute and significant mental health needs should be referred to local services as early as possible to receive individual, specialised input.

WHO THIS BOOK IS FOR

This book is designed for any professional working with children and teens on the autism spectrum in a range of settings and contexts.

- Teachers (primary and secondary)

- Further education tutors

- Special/Additional educational needs co-ordinators (SENCOs/ALNCOs)

- Teaching assistants

- Specialist SEN teachers

- School pastoral staff

- Inclusion mentors

- Speech and language therapists

- Social workers

- Family support workers

- Counsellors

- Therapists

- Mentors

- School nurses

- Specialist autism mentors

- Health professionals

Parents and carers of children and young people on the autism spectrum will also find this book useful. The strategies in this book will have the most impact when all of the adults involved with the child or young person are using them consistently. Each section of the book contains:

- **Group activities.** These are designed for mainstream classrooms or small group work in a range of contexts. It is recognised that children and young people on the autism spectrum are likely to be educated in mainstream environments and will not always have access to autism-specific groups. Therefore the group activities are designed to be beneficial to any child or young person, while being fully inclusive of those on the autism spectrum. Guidance is provided for overcoming particular challenges that individuals on the autism spectrum may face. These activities are all suitable for mainstream classrooms, youth groups, support groups or any other group setting.

- **Individual activities.** Designed for use with individual children and teens on the autism spectrum in a range of settings (schools, health, community and home).

- **Adult communication.** Strategies for any adult working with children and young people on the autism spectrum whether at school, in the community or at home.

No prior training in psychology is required in order to deliver the activities in this book; they are designed to be used by a range of professionals and parents. The most important skills you can bring to working with autistic young people are an open mind, a calm presence and a willingness to accept difference. If you would like to find out more about positive psychology and emotional wellbeing you may find it useful to seek further training; a list of further resources is included at the end of this book.

The autism spectrum is, by its very nature, a spectrum, and encompasses a huge range of individuals who are affected in different ways and to different levels of severity. An increasing number of young people also have additional difficulties or diagnoses. As a result, the activities and strategies in this book may not necessarily be suitable for all children and young people with a diagnosis of an autism spectrum condition. They have been designed predominantly to meet the needs of children and young people on the autism spectrum who are able to communicate verbally and who are educated in mainstream primary and secondary school environments (especially those with Asperger Syndrome/Autism Spectrum Disorder Level 1). The activities can, however, all be adapted to meet individual interests and abilities. Many of the activities will also be of benefit to a wide range of young people with various needs, not only those on the autism spectrum; do not be too limited by labels and diagnoses. If you feel a child or young person would benefit, then put the strategy into place. It is often stated that good practice for those on the autism spectrum is, in fact, good practice for all students.

This book is designed to be used with children and young people roughly between the ages of 7 and 18, although some individuals outside this age bracket may also benefit. Some activities are more suitable for the younger end of this age group while others are more suitable for the older end. Recommended age groups for each activity have been included after the activity title, although most activities can be easily adapted for older or younger children. Age groups have been divided roughly into corresponding 'Key Stages' in the UK education system: ages 7–11 (Key Stage 2), ages 11–14 (Key Stage 3), ages 14–16 (Key Stage 4), ages 16–18 (Key Stage 5).

HOW TO USE THIS BOOK

This book is split into sections which can be read independently of each other. You may like to 'dip in' to the chapters which you find most relevant to the young people you are working with. Each chapter begins with a brief introduction to the topic and its relevance, followed by group activities, individual activities and adult communication strategies. The book is not designed to be an intervention to be delivered in a set order, but as a collection of activities to choose from and use as and when the opportunity occurs. How you choose to deliver the activities will depend upon the time and resources you have available.

To gain a better understanding of positive psychology and why it is an appropriate approach to use with individuals on the autism spectrum, you are recommended to read Chapters 2 and 3. For readers looking for a shorter overview, the first chapter, 'If You Only Have Five Minutes…', contains a brief overview of the book.

TERMINOLOGY

There are many arguments for and against using certain terminology when it comes to discussing the autism spectrum. Some individuals prefer identity-first language (*an autistic person*), while others prefer people-first language (*a person with autism*).

Diagnostic labels have also changed in recent years. 'Asperger Syndrome', 'High Functioning Autism', 'PDD-NOS' and several other separate diagnoses now all come under the umbrella of 'autism'. Under the newest diagnostic criteria of the DSM-5 (Diagnostic and Statistical Manual of Mental Disorders of the American Psychiatric Association, 5th edition), individuals on the autism spectrum receive a diagnosis of 'Autism Spectrum Disorder Level 1/2/3', depending on the severity of their autism and the impact it has on their daily life.

In this book the term 'on the autism spectrum' is used to refer to all individuals on the autism spectrum, including those who identify with the 'Asperger Syndrome' or 'High Functioning Autism' diagnosis. 'Autism Spectrum Conditions' (ASC) is also used as opposed to 'Autism Spectrum Disorders' (ASD) to reflect the belief that autism is neither a deficit, disease nor disorder, but simply a different, and equally valid, way of being.

For ease the term 'students' is used to refer to all children and young people, although these activities can all be delivered just as successfully in non-educational settings. Equally the term 'classroom' is used to refer to any setting or environment.

CHAPTER OVERVIEW

Chapter 1, 'If You Only Have Five Minutes…', briefly summarises the main points of this book and signposts busy readers to key topics and activities.

Chapter 2, 'Understanding the Autism Spectrum' provides an overview of the autism spectrum. You will find out about the origins of autism, diagnostic criteria and about the autism spectrum. You will also explore some of the differences that individuals on the autism spectrum can experience. Finally, you will learn more about working with children and young people on the autism spectrum, including some key points to take into consideration, strategies for 'active listening' and how to cope with common challenges.

In Chapter 3, 'Understanding Positive Psychology' you will learn about positive psychology. You will find out about the key people and concepts covered by this branch of psychology. Some of the main research findings of this movement are discussed. You will also explore the potential benefits of using a positive psychology approach with individuals on the autism spectrum to support them in achieving greater levels of happiness and wellbeing.

In Chapter 4, 'Recognising, Identifying and Using Character Strengths' you will discover what is meant by the term 'character strengths'. What are character strengths and how can we benefit from recognising and utilising them? Explore how individuals who use their character strengths are happier and how you can support young people on the autism spectrum in identifying their own character strengths.

The next chapter of the book, Chapter 5, 'Cultivating Positive Emotions', identifies various positive emotions and investigates how these can be promoted and cultivated.

In the section 'Happiness, joy and inspiration' you will reflect on what is meant by 'happiness', a word we use every day but that can be very difficult to define. What makes somebody happy? Can happiness be taught? Can we improve our happiness levels? And why can it be difficult for autistic individuals to experience 'happiness'?

You will explore activities which can help young people on the autism spectrum to increase their happiness levels.

'Hope and optimism' are two further positive emotions which can improve wellbeing. In this section you will discover tasks and activities which can support young people on the autism spectrum to develop hope and optimism through developing more positive ways of thinking, goal-setting techniques and problem-solving strategies.

'Flow' is a state identified by psychologist Mikhail Csikszent-mihalyi, and describes the sense of deep engagement in an activity. This section explores the benefits and difficulties for young people on the autism spectrum in experiencing 'flow', and how to promote other optimal experiences.

In the 'Gratitude and appreciation' section we investigate why grateful people are happier than their not-as-grateful counterparts and possible barriers that exist for autistic individuals to experience gratitude. You will consider how you can develop feelings of gratitude and appreciation in the young people you work with.

Positive psychology is not just about increasing positive emotions and ignoring those we feel are less positive, rather it is about learning how to cope more positively with these other, perhaps less helpful emotions. The last chapter of the book considers 'Positive Coping'.

First, you will consider what is meant by 'Resilience'. Why is resilience important and can it be taught? How do young people develop resilience, why can some young people on the autism spectrum find this difficult and why is it particularly important for autistic individuals to be resilient?

Next you will explore what is meant by a 'Growth mindset'. In a growth mindset people believe that their talents and abilities can be developed through dedication and hard work. This chapter explores activities and strategies which can be used to support young people on the autism spectrum to overcome any challenges they can experience in developing a growth mindset.

In 'Wellbeing' you will learn about scientifically proven evidence that increases wellbeing levels. We discuss possible challenges for individuals on the autism spectrum and explore strategies that can be implemented to increase the wellbeing levels of children and young people.

Finally, in 'Meaning and purpose' we discuss why positive psychology also concerns itself with these wider issues. We explore the benefits of developing 'meaning and purpose' in young people and suggest tasks and activities which can support this.

At the end of the book you will find a Glossary of key terms relating to the themes in this book and a list of Further Reading and Resources for those wanting to investigate further.

The Appendices include printable resources to be used in the activities, and they are available to download and print from www.jkp.com/voucher using the code HONEYBOURNEHAPPINESS.

1

IF YOU ONLY HAVE FIVE MINUTES...

WHAT IS AUTISM?

Autism is a spectrum condition which affects people in different ways and to different levels of severity. Some individuals on the autism spectrum may be of average or above average intelligence, while others may have associated learning difficulties, may require alternative methods of communication and will need support with everyday living tasks.

Individuals on the autism spectrum interpret the world differently, connect to others in a different way and can find other people confusing and unpredictable. Being on the autism spectrum has been likened to being a computer with a different operating system to the majority – your brain is simply hardwired a different way. Those on the autism spectrum experience differences in two main areas: social communication and interaction, and restricted and repetitive patterns of behaviours, activities or interests.

WHAT ARE THE DIFFICULTIES?

Living in a world which has not been designed for their ways of thinking, learning and relating to others can be difficult for those on the autism spectrum. Research suggests that young people on the autism spectrum can be more likely that their peers to experience mental health difficulties such as depression, anxiety and worry. They also often experience lower self-esteem and self-worth, may have fewer friendships, and may be more vulnerable to peer pressure or bullying. Feeling misunderstood can also be problematic and unfortunately many autistic individuals report negative experiences of education, employment and community participation.

INTRODUCING POSITIVE PSYCHOLOGY

Psychology has traditionally focused on the more negative aspects of human life, such as mental illness and disorders. The branch of positive psychology, however, focuses on more positive human experiences such as wellbeing, happiness, human strengths, resilience and flourishing. Positive psychology is the scientific study of these aspects of human existence and is developing a solid evidence base of how to increase and develop these positive experiences and attitudes. Although the field of positive psychology has expanded enormously over the past two decades, relatively little evidence exists about how to apply the findings to individuals on the autism spectrum. This book aims to add to the literature by suggesting challenges and opportunities for children and young people on the autism spectrum when using a positive psychology approach.

WHERE TO START IF...

...you are looking for strategies to use in a mainstream classroom or larger group which may not exclusively be made up of children and young people on the autism spectrum.

- Check out the 'Group activities' section of each chapter. Remember too to read the 'Adult communication' section in each chapter.

...you are working with a small group of children and young people on the autism spectrum (or with similar difficulties).

- Look at the 'Group activities' section of each chapter. Some of the 'Individual activities' can also be used with small groups of students, and remember to read the 'Adult communication' section too.

…you have one-to-one time with a child or young person on the autism spectrum.

- Read the 'Individual activities' and 'Adult communication' section of each chapter.

…you teach or support students on the autism spectrum in the classroom or other settings but do not necessarily have dedicated time set aside to work on wellbeing.

- Start with the 'Adult communication' section of each chapter. Even just putting these small changes into place can make a big difference. Scan the 'Group activities' and 'Individual activities' as there may also be opportunities to use some of these in your role, or to adapt existing opportunities.

…you are a parent or carer of a child or young person on the autism spectrum.

- Start by reading the 'Adult communication' section of each chapter – this can often make a big difference to children and young people on the autism spectrum. Next read the 'Individual activities' sections of each chapter and decide which are most suitable for your child.

2

UNDERSTANDING THE AUTISM SPECTRUM

THE AUTISM SPECTRUM

Autism spectrum conditions were first identified in the 1940s, although individuals with these characteristics have undoubtedly existed throughout human history. Autism comes from the Greek word *autos*, meaning 'self'. This reflects the fact that autistic individuals do not connect with other people in the same way as others do. Autistic people can appear quite self-contained or self-reliant, not connecting instinctively with others. Autism has been described by some as not having the innate capacity to connect on a social level, or having a 'social blindness' (Weldon 2014). Some autistic individuals may feel no desire to connect with other people, while others may wish to, but find that they connect differently.

Autism is not a physical disability, nor is it a mental illness. It is a lifelong condition and currently thought to affect more than 1 in 100 people in the United Kingdom (National Autistic Society (NAS) 2016a). The exact causes of autism are not yet known, but it is thought to have a genetic basis. Autism is something that individuals are born with, it is not something caused by upbringing or that is developed in later life.

Autism is now seen as a different way of being, rather than as a 'disorder', as a 'spectrum' of conditions with individuals being affected to different degrees. Some individuals on the autism spectrum may be very capable and intelligent in some areas; they might be able to live independently, have professional level jobs or even be experts in their chosen fields. These individuals may have fewer obvious difficulties with language and communication but will still experience significant differences in the way that they connect and relate to others, as well as in how they interpret the world. Other individuals on the autism spectrum may have associated learning difficulties or may be non-verbal, communicating in ways other than using speech. These individuals may need a high level of lifelong care and support. However, all individuals on the autism spectrum share differences in two main areas:

- social communication and interaction

- restricted and repetitive patterns of behaviours, activities or interests (including sensory behaviour).

DIFFICULTIES AND DIFFERENCES EXPERIENCED BY THOSE ON THE AUTISM SPECTRUM
Social communication and interaction

Difficulties can include:

- feelings of being different and not connecting to others, not having the instinctive ability to 'connect' that others seem to have

- interpreting and using verbal language (may have a literal understanding, difficulty interpreting jokes or sarcasm)

- interpreting non-verbal language (tone of voice, gesture, body language, facial expression)

- understanding the expectations of conversation (e.g. talking at length about their own interests, repeating what the other person has said (echolalia), difficulty maintaining or staying on topic)

- following the dynamics of group conversation

- recognising and understanding the thoughts and feelings of other people (also called 'theory of mind')

- recognising, understanding and expressing their own feelings (also called 'alexithymia')

- forming friendships and relationships

- appearing different to others (e.g. may appear insensitive, may prefer their own company, may not seek comfort from others in expected ways, may appear socially inappropriate)

- feeling overwhelmed by the social world and social interaction

- understanding and following social 'norms'.

Restricted and repetitive patterns of behaviours, activities or interests

Difficulties and differences can include:

- using restricted and repetitive routines to help overcome the difficulties of living in an uncomfortable and unpredictable world

- relying on 'rules'

- finding it difficult to cope with change or new experiences

- having intense and highly focused interests (often called 'special interests')

- sensory processing differences (see below).

Further differences

In addition, it is recognised that many individuals on the autism spectrum also experience sensory difficulties. Individuals may be hypo- (under-) or hyper- (over-) sensitive to various sensory inputs.

SENSORY INPUTS

Vision

Undersensitive: Enjoys bright lights and movement; objects appear dark or lose their features. Objects appear blurred.

Oversensitive: Prefers dimmer light, overwhelmed by too much light (especially fluorescent lighting), complex patterns or too many visual distractions.

Sound

Undersensitive: Might only hear certain sounds, or sounds in one ear. Might like loud noises.

Oversensitive: Noise can appear amplified (a loud voice can be interpreted as shouting, the hum of a computer can be over-whelming). Difficulties in eliminating background noise and being able to concentrate on a conversation.

Smell

Undersensitive: May have no sense of smell and fail to identify smells (including their own body odour).

Oversensitive: Smells can be intense and overpowering. May dislike people wearing certain perfumes or deodorants.

Taste

Undersensitive: May like very spicy food or may eat everything – for example, soil, grass, Play-Doh.

Oversensitive: Finds some foods and flavours overpowering due to sensitive taste buds. Certain textures cause discomfort.

Touch

Undersensitive: Needs to hold others tightly before there is a sensation of having applied any pressure. High pain threshold. Enjoys heavy objects on top of them such as weighted blankets.

Oversensitive: Touch can be painful – might have a strong dislike of other people touching them. May dislike having things on hands, feet or head. Some fabrics can feel painful or 'scratchy'.

Vestibular system

The vestibular system helps us to maintain balance and tells us how fast our body is moving.

Undersensitive: May need to rock, swing or spin.

Oversensitive: May have difficulty with controlling body movement or car sickness.

Proprioception

Proprioception is our body awareness system which integrates information about the position and movement of our body in space. Difficulties for individuals on the autism spectrum may include standing too close to people, standing too far away, bumping into things, needing to lean on things, or difficulty with fine motor skills.

AN AUTISM DIAGNOSIS

Autism is usually diagnosed by a multidisciplinary team, often made up of psychiatrists, psychologists, paediatricians and speech and language therapists. Many professionals use the American Psychiatric Association's *Diagnostic and Statistical Manual, fifth edition* (DSM-5; 2013) to diagnose. The latest edition of this manual has removed some terms which were given in the past as separate diagnoses (such as 'Asperger Syndrome', 'High Functioning Autism' or 'PDD-NOS'). Individuals are now all given a diagnosis of 'Autism Spectrum Disorder' on a sliding scale of 'severity' depending on how far the condition impacts on everyday life for the individual in question:

Autism Spectrum Disorder Level 1: Requiring support (individuals with 'Asperger Syndrome' would usually fit this category)

Autism Spectrum Disorder Level 2: Requiring significant support

Autism Spectrum Disorder Level 3: Requiring very substantial support

Are there differences between males and females on the autism spectrum?

Traditionally, autism was considered by many to be a 'male' condition and many more males were diagnosed than females. Participants in original autism research of the 1940s had mainly been male and diagnostic criteria had developed out of this. Media portrayals of autism had also generally reflected these male presentations of autism (such as in the film *Rainman* and the book *The Curious Incident of the Dog in the Night Time*). It is now recognised, however, that just as many females may be affected by autism as males. The difference is that they might often cope with their autism differently, making it harder to identify. There is currently much research going on in this area, but some possible differences identified so far include:

- Females on the autism spectrum are more likely to 'mask', hide or camouflage their difficulties. They might be more able to copy and mimic others, hiding some of their difficulties with social interaction (Hurley 2014). Their differences may, therefore, be less obvious to observers.

- Boys may respond to their difficulties with more challenging behaviour (Hurley 2014) while girls may internalise their difficulties (Solomon *et al.* 2012), leading to mental health difficulties such as depression or anxiety. Again, difficulties may be less noticed.

- Girls on the autism spectrum may show less restricted and repetitive patterns of behaviour than boys on the autism spectrum (Van Wijngaarden-Cremers *et al.* 2014).

- Whereas boys may have special interests which are unusual and stand out, girls' special interests may be similar to their neurotypical peers; the difference is the intensity and dominance of these interests (Gould and Ashton-Smith 2011).

- Girls may develop 'coping strategies' which hide their difficulties (Attwood 2007).

- Females on the autism spectrum may be more open to talking about their feelings and may be more expressive in gesture, tone of voice and facial expression than males on the autism spectrum (Simone 2010).

TOP TIP! Remember that the central characteristics of autism are still the same in males and females – there will still be significant differences in social communication and interaction – it is simply how some females may cope with these difficulties that is different.

Autism and other conditions

Autism can occur with or without additional psychological conditions and disabilities. Other difficulties which can also often occur in individuals on the autism spectrum can include conditions such as general learning difficulties, attention deficit hyperactivity disorder (ADHD), dyslexia or dyspraxia.

NEURODIVERSITY AND OTHER THEORIES

There are many different ways of viewing autism. Some people view it as a 'disorder', whereas others see it simply as a different way of being, one which is equally as valid as any other way of being.

Models of disability

Using the medical model of disability, autism is classed as a 'disorder', something wrong within the individual which needs to be treated, 'fixed' or cured. A social model of disability, however, implies that individuals are only disabled by the society around them, that environments, policies and practices put some individuals (such as those on the autism spectrum) at a disadvantage; it is society that needs to change to become more inclusive.

KEY TERMS

Neurodiversity. The diversity of ways in which humans think, learn and relate to others (in the same way as we have cultural diversity, gender diversity or biodiversity).

The neurodiversity paradigm. The neurodiversity paradigm views these differences in neurocognitive functioning as a normal, and expected, part of human variation. No one way of functioning is considered to be superior to any other.

This book uses the neurodiversity paradigm as the underpinning theoretical approach. The autistic way of being is not considered inferior to any other way, nor is it seen as something that needs to be fixed. This is not a book about making young people on the autism spectrum more 'normal', rather about helping them to be happy and confident to be themselves. There is also a focus on changing attitudes of those around them to be more accepting of the wonderful diversity of human life.

DIFFICULTIES IN EDUCATIONAL ENVIRONMENTS FOR CHILDREN AND YOUNG PEOPLE ON THE AUTISM SPECTRUM

Many children and young people on the autism spectrum are educated in mainstream school environments. Some achieve very well at school and some positive aspects of the school experience reported by individuals on the autism spectrum include:

- being academically able in one or more subjects

- having a thirst for knowledge

- having a good memory for facts and figures

- being hard working and conscientious

- enjoying the routine and structure of having a timetable

- following rules and instructions accurately

- being creative and able to see things from a more unusual perspective

- taking part in extracurricular activities related to their special interest

- benefiting from having supportive teachers and peers.

However, many children and young people on the autism spectrum also experience some difficulties in the school or college environment. These can include:

- finding social times (break and lunchtimes) difficult due to the lack of structure and emphasis on spending time with friends; many find it difficult to connect with and socialise with peers

- having difficulty making and maintaining friendships

- preferring (and needing) to spend time alone but not having the opportunity to do so

- finding group work difficult

- difficulties keeping up with and joining in group conversation in the classroom

- difficulties in understanding the perspectives of staff and peers; frustration with other people

- taking things literally – instructions, information and sayings. finding inference difficult (when listening and reading)

- differences in ways of communication (such as finding eye contact uncomfortable) and getting into trouble because of this

- needing additional processing time to make sense of information

- not understanding why rules are not applied fairly and consistently

- sensory discomfort due to noisy environments, crowds of people, artificial lighting, smells, textures and too much information

- difficulties with personal organisation and executive functioning tasks (e.g. planning and organising, shifting attention from one task to another)

- low self-esteem and confidence

- constant feelings of anxiety about the school day

- feelings of worry, depression or isolation due to 'not fitting in'

- needing support to access the mainstream school but at the same time not wanting to feel any more different than they already do

- being vulnerable to peer pressure or bullying.

These are by no means exhaustive lists, and what should be remembered above all is that no two individuals on the autism spectrum will have identical strengths and difficulties.

WORKING WITH CHILDREN AND YOUNG PEOPLE ON THE AUTISM SPECTRUM

As you encounter more and more individuals on the autism spectrum, you will soon find that no two respond in exactly the same way, just as no two non-autistic students are the same. Children and young people on the autism spectrum are all affected by autism differently, may or may not have other difficulties and needs, and have different backgrounds, life experiences and networks. Therefore, what works with one student may not work with another student; what is difficult for one may be straightforward for another. The best things you can bring to your work with autistic students are an open mind and a willingness to get to know individuals. In addition, the list below highlights some general points to take into consideration.

- **Timing is key.** Many of the activities in this book require students to reflect on themselves, their feelings or on their past experiences in an open and non-judgemental manner. It is almost impossible to do this if in a state of anxiety, anger or frustration. Try to schedule any sessions at a time when students are able to get the most out of the work. If children have just had a meltdown or major argument with friends or family then they are unlikely to be able to concentrate. Try to choose times when participants are feeling calm and relaxed. If they are worried about something else, it can be a good idea to alleviate the worry first and return to these activities once the issue has been resolved.

- **Beware hunger and tiredness gremlins!** It can also be very difficult to focus when hungry, thirsty or tired. Arrange sessions when this is less likely to be a problem for students, or provide a healthy snack and drink before the session. Hunger and tiredness can also affect adults' enthusiasm, so don't forget to monitor your own needs too!

- **Eliminate distractions in the environment.** School classrooms and other settings can be busy, noisy environments with frequent interruptions and distractions. Once focus is lost, it can take considerable time to reorient attention on a task. Some studies even indicate that this reorientation to an original activity can take anywhere between 5 and 25 minutes (Kutscher 2016). Use a comfortable room and assemble any resources needed in advance. Turn off any digital devices and place a sign on the door requesting no interruptions.

- **Set ground rules.** All children and young people will respond best to clear and consistent expectations, and these are especially important for young people on the autism spectrum. Give any 'rules' at the beginning of the session and explain why these are in place. Reiterate these expectations when necessary and calmly explain the importance of them.

You could try creating a 'group agreement' in the first session to which all group members contribute and then sign. You might like to include agreements such as 'We will respect other people's opinions,' 'We will not interrupt when another person is talking,' or 'We will keep things discussed in our group confidential.'

- **Consider sensory differences.** Many children and young people on the autism spectrum also experience sensory sensitivities. These will vary from individual to individual. Being overwhelmed by sensory input can increase anxiety and frustration in individuals, making it harder to focus and to concentrate. At a more extreme level, some individuals may find it so hard to cope that they 'shut down' or 'melt down'. Be aware that background noise (such as people whispering or talking) can be disturbing for some young people on the autism spectrum, as can bright, fluorescent lighting or crowds of people. Try to choose a calm and quiet place to work which has a neutral décor and comfortable ambience.

Communicating with students on the autism spectrum

The activities in this book have no right or wrong answers. Young people's thoughts, feelings, opinions, hopes and dreams are all very individual and each student will respond to the tasks in different ways. Sometimes it can be easy for adults to 'jump in' and tell a young person what they must be thinking or feeling. However, this is not conducive to young people developing self-awareness and self-acceptance, and, indeed, can lead to some young people feeling misunderstood. This can be particularly relevant for young people on the autism spectrum. Some report that their feelings have often been mislabelled by adults, resulting in them perceiving that they must somehow be 'wrong' and believing that their feelings are unacceptable.

DANGERS OF MISLABELLING FEELINGS

Susan was due to attend a classmate's birthday party which has been cancelled at the last minute. 'Oh, you must be feeling so disappointed!' her teacher tells her. Susan is confused. She was not feeling disappointed at all, in fact, she was feeling quite relieved! She had not been looking forward to the party and is now happy that she can spend the evening finishing a painting. Was she meant to feel disappointed? Why did she not feel this? Is it not ok to feel relieved?

Active listening

It is important to listen and respond to students in an open and non-judgmental manner. One method of doing this is that of 'active listening'.

How to do it

The concept of 'active listening' is often referred to in counselling and psychotherapy but it is a useful strategy for anybody to use to improve their listening skills.

- **Show that you are listening.** Be aware of any messages that your body language might be giving. Ensure that your facial expression, posture and gestures are open and relaxed.

- **Avoid distractions in the environment.** Fidgeting, looking at your watch or clock, glancing at your phone, typing while talking: these are all actions which suggest to the talker that your focus is not on them.

- **Be mindful of distracting thoughts.** Children and young people, especially those on the autism spectrum, can be very perceptive about whether adults are really 'present' or not. Try to avoid any internal distractions of your own so that you can also focus on the session. Make a mental note if you feel your attention wandering ('What's for dinner this evening? I really must call into the grocery store on my way home'), and bring your attention back to the present moment. It can be very easy to let our thoughts wander when listening and, before we know it, we have lost track of what is being said.

- **Try not to plan your response while the talker is speaking.** Try instead to focus carefully on the words that are being used. If you are planning what you are going to say next, your attention is not completely on what is being said.

- **Ask questions to clarify points.** If you really have not understood, then do not pretend. Be honest and ask the student to repeat what they have said to you, or ask them if they could help you to understand by explaining further.

- **Avoid using 'why'.** Too many 'why' questions can begin to sound like an interrogation! 'Why' questions can also be perceived at times to be blaming or criticising. Use other question words instead or, even better, use comments rather than questions to avoid the conversation sounding like an interrogation.

- **Use a calm and neutral tone of voice.** This is especially important when working with young people on the autism spectrum as many can have heightened sensory sensitivities, or can have difficulty in interpreting tone of voice. Speaking in a loud voice, for example, may come across as shouting or being angry. 'Overenthusiasm' could be perceived as being 'fake' or patronising.

- **Accept what is said without commenting, judging or criticising.** This can be difficult, especially if you have strong opinions of your own or if you believe the other person is wrong. Remember, you do not have to agree with the other person, just try to avoid any intentional, or unintentional, judgement or criticism.

- **Avoid asking leading questions.** Try not to put words into the student's mouth. Questions such as 'And then what happened – you went to report the accident to the teacher?' invite the young person to agree, as do questions such as 'Swimming is so boring, isn't it?'

- **Occasionally reflect back what the speaker is saying, or summarise the main points.** Try to use the speaker's own words when possible.

Dealing with difficulties

Working with children and young people is no easy task and there will often be times when they do not respond to activities in the way that you had hoped or expected. Children and young people on the autism spectrum in particular may respond in different than expected ways and their behaviour and responses may sometimes appear confusing on the surface. There are no hard and fast rules about what to do in such situations, as no two young people on the autism spectrum are alike; the best advice is to treat each student as an individual, get to know them and accept their views and opinions with an open mind. In addition, parents, carers and staff who have worked with students previously can be useful sources of information and will be able to tell you more about effective strategies for each student. Some general points to take into consideration are listed below:

The student who doesn't want to be there

There can be different reasons for this:

Worries, concerns and anxieties

Is the student worried or concerned about something else, meaning they are unable to concentrate? Students on the autism spectrum in particular may find it difficult to focus on anything else, as their worry and resulting anxiety can be overwhelming. When you get to the root of the problem, the issue itself may seem relatively insignificant, but do not underestimate the impact this minor worry may have had on the student. Some students on the autism spectrum can find it difficult to filter out unimportant details (Young 2009), may take things literally, and may have difficulty in understanding other people or in predicting social behaviour. All of these things can mean 'getting the wrong end of the stick' and worrying about something which may not be a problem for the other people involved. In addition, students on the autism spectrum can take longer than others to process and understand their own emotions (Rowe 2015). This means that a student may still be processing something which has happened a few hours, days or even weeks before. It may seem a delayed or over-reaction to onlookers, but for the student involved emotions can still be just as raw as when the event occurred.

What to do: If the problem can be solved easily, then help the student to solve it before expecting them to engage in another activity. That way they can focus their attention on the task in hand and eliminate their anxieties. Other strategies which may be suitable for different students include:

- talking the problem through, helping the student to put it in perspective

- setting a fixed time when the student can speak to somebody about the issue in more depth – write this in your diary and the student's planner so that they know it will definitely happen

- creating a quick written action plan to help the student to break down the problem into small steps and know what they are able to do about it

- asking the student to write it down or draw the problem so that it is out of their head and explain that they can talk it through with an adult later

- comic strip conversations or social stories may help some students to make sense of events or prepare for new ones (Gray 2015)

- relaxation techniques such as focusing on breathing or colouring in for a few moments can help to reduce immediate anxiety.

Changes to routine

Changes to routine can upset us all – just think about how you felt the last time you came across some unexpected roadworks, had to take a detour, got lost and ended up late! Students on the autism spectrum can find changes particularly difficult to cope with. This may be a problem if students are asked to complete these activities in place of their usual timetable, or if students have been taken out of a class to work on an intervention.

What to do: Prepare students for any changes in advance by explaining what the student will be doing, where this will take place, how long it will last and why the students are taking part. Show your enthusiasm and focus on the positives. Also ensure that students are not removed from their favourite lessons in order to complete any interventions or group work. Although you may recognise the importance of the new activities for the student, they may resent being taken from a favourite activity, or may worry about missing out, so that this outweighs any benefits they may get.

Not seeing the point

Some students on the autism spectrum can experience some rigidity of thought and they might not see the 'point' of completing activities which are not directly necessary to them passing their exams – this might be what they consider to be the 'point' of school.

What to do: Explain calmly and clearly the importance and relevance of activities. Link taking part to a student's individual hopes and targets – if, for example, a student has previously identified that they want to get better at biology to pursue a medical career then you may be able to explain the benefits of the 'growth mindset' activities in those terms – developing a 'growth mindset' will help the student to reach their personal goals. Be aware too of the messages students may be getting from other staff in the setting and at home – if there is a great emphasis on exam results and they are told repeatedly that that is the most important thing, students on the autism spectrum are likely to take this very literally.

Disruptive behaviour

'Disruptive' behaviour can occur for many reasons and even small issues such as arriving late to a lesson or not having the correct equipment can disrupt other students' learning and the flow of the lesson. On a larger scale, disruptive behaviours may include shouting out, interruptions, refusal to work, arguing with others or trying to stop other students from working. In addition, students on the autism spectrum can be over- or under-sensitive to sensory stimuli which can sometimes be problematic when working in a classroom environment. Some students, for example, may be unable to work if they can hear another student breathing, may get distressed by certain smells, may prefer to work in the dark or may be unable to focus if there is background noise. These sensitivities may then trigger emotional outbursts or inappropriate behaviour.

What to do: Again, the best advice is to get to know individual students so that you are able to mitigate any sensory sensitivities which may occur. As students become older, help them to identify their own sensory preferences and to develop coping strategies which work for them (e.g. wearing thin gloves when working with glue, wearing tinted glasses in bright lights, moving themselves to a quieter corner of the classroom). In addition, it can be useful to audit your classroom or work space and consider how 'autism friendly' it is. Perhaps you can alter lighting levels, remove distractions, tidy up or create some quieter work areas. There is more information about autism-friendly environments in the 'Wellbeing' section of Chapter 6.

Inappropriate comments

Some of the activities in this book require personal responses; students are asked to reflect on themselves and on what is meaningful to them as individuals. It is important that students feel that they are in a safe, open-minded and non-judgemental environment so that they are able to express themselves freely. Some students may make inappropriate comments which can be offensive, hurtful or damaging to others in the group. Some students on the autism spectrum may not realise the impact of their words on others due to difficulties with theory of mind (understanding things from others' perspectives).

What to do: Set 'ground rules' in advance for the sessions and refer to these at the beginning of each session. Perhaps display them prominently in the room to refer to. Include the importance of respecting other people's point of view and of not interrupting.

There are some comments which are unacceptable (e.g. racist language, sexist terms, obscenities and derogatory terms) and your setting is likely to have clear guidelines on what to do in these situations. However, it is important to explain to students why the term they have used is unacceptable (some students may not know why and are simply repeating something they have heard others use).

Other comments may be inappropriate rather than unacceptable (e.g. saying something which is tactless). In those cases, it is best to explain to the student in question why the comment was inappropriate and explain the effect it may have had on the other person. Help the student to think about alternative words or phrases to use in future situations. Remember that your attitude can make all the difference – showing understanding and being supportive is likely to have a far more beneficial effect than appearing angry and imposing a sanction without explanation.

Irrelevant comments

You might encounter students who make seemingly irrelevant comments. Perhaps they go off on a tangent, 'hog the air time' or talk at length about topics which have no relation to what you would like the group to be talking about! This can be frustrating as you may begin to worry about getting through your activities, may be concerned that they have not got the 'point' of the lesson and may worry that other students will also be confused! Sometimes it can be difficult to know how to get students back on task, while not wanting them to feel they are being brushed aside or not listened to.

What to do: To some students on the autism spectrum, their comments may not be as irrelevant as they may appear. Individuals on the autism spectrum can sometimes have difficulty in expressing themselves clearly and may also experience difficulty with giving too much or too little information – they may assume that the listener knows some key information which in fact they do not!

Support the student to explain their thinking, perhaps prompting them to return to the question or asking them directly to relate what they are saying to the topic in question. If a student talks too much, be honest (but polite) with them; explain that, out of fairness, every student needs to have a chance to respond to the question so, although what they are saying is very interesting, unfortunately you are going to have to cut them short, but they can talk to you, or another adult, later in the lesson.

Alternatively try providing a sentence starter (e.g. 'I feel happy when…') that students have to use to begin their answers – this may help some to give a more relevant response.

Some students may benefit from being taught explicitly how to summarise their thoughts and pick out the key information. This can also be done with the whole group as it is a useful skill for all students. Try setting a challenge – every student has to respond in five sentences or less (no 'ands' allowed!), or a student has to summarise another student's thoughts in just five key words.

Some students may just want to talk about something else which is irrelevant to the topic in question, but probably very interesting to them as an individual. Different tactics may be required in this case. Some students may respond to being given a set time when they can talk about their interest. Allocate ten minutes at the end of a lesson when they can talk to an adult about their interest. Make this visual on a visual timetable, workboard or on a written list of activities and make sure it happens if you have promised it.

This chapter has not been written to provide a complete overview of the autism spectrum, but merely to highlight some of the key points for professionals working with children and young people. For more detailed information see the 'Further Reading and Resources' section of this book.

3

UNDERSTANDING POSITIVE PSYCHOLOGY

WHAT IS POSITIVE PSYCHOLOGY?

The discipline of psychology has traditionally been focused on deficits, difficulties and disorders, examining the more negative aspects of human life. For many people, the term psychology is synonymous with mental illness and psychologists are those tasked with understanding and curing these 'diseases and disorders'.

However, since the turn of the twenty-first century a new movement has been gathering momentum, that of 'positive psychology'. Rather than delving into the negatives and the 'what's gone wrong?' positive psychology instead investigates the more positive aspects of human existence: positive emotions, human resourcefulness and resilience, strengths, talents and flourishing, at both an individual and collective level. In the words of the movement's founder, Martin Seligman, positive psychology is summarised as the 'scientific study of optimal human functioning that aims to discover and promote the factors that allow individuals and communities to thrive' (Seligman and Csikszentmihalyi 2000, p.5).

KEY PEOPLE

Martin Seligman. Psychologist seen as the 'founder' of the positive psychology movement.

Mikhail Csikszentmihalyi. Another key positive psychologist who named and explored the theory of 'flow', total engagement in an activity that brings intrinsic enjoyment.

Positive psychology is now a rapidly expanding field and aims to bring solid, scientific, empirical research evidence to the study of happiness and wellbeing. Many ideas from positive psychology are beginning to move into mainstream culture, and governments and other large organisations are using findings from the movement to influence policy and practice.

WHAT DOES POSITIVE PSYCHOLOGY COVER?

- Positive emotions
- Happiness
- Life satisfaction
- Wellbeing
- Optimism
- Hope
- Creativity
- Flow
- Strengths and virtues
- Wisdom
- Courage
- Emotional intelligence

- Self-esteem
- Positive coping
- Resilience
- Motivation
- Achieving goals
- Coaching
- Positive relationships
- Positive therapy
- Positive education
- Wellbeing at work
- Positive parenting

WHAT HAS POSITIVE PSYCHOLOGY TOLD US SO FAR?

Positive psychology as a discipline has developed quickly and new findings are constantly being added to the body of knowledge. Go into any large bookstore and you will find rows of books on related topics! Some of the main findings so far have suggested:

- Happiness levels tend to decrease in middle life, with people in their 20s and 60s being happier than those in between (Office for National Statistics 2016).

- Being grateful and having feelings of gratitude tend to increase happiness (Emmons 2007; Lyubomirsky 2007).

- Positive emotional states can have a positive impact on physical health (Boniwell and Ryan 2012).

- Conversely, people who perceive themselves as having good physical health are happier than those who perceive themselves as being in poor health (Office for National Statistics 2016).

- Money does not seem to increase happiness as much as enjoying your job or having a supportive social network (Easterlin 2008).

- Using our strengths can increase feelings of happiness and wellbeing (Boniwell 2015).

- 'Flow' is a positive emotional state which increases wellbeing (Csikszentmihalyi 1992).

- Resilience and a growth mindset can be developed in individuals (Dweck 2006).

Positive psychologists have also identified ten 'keys' to happier living (Rae 2016). These are ten scientifically proven things that can increase happiness levels. They make the acronym GREAT DREAM.

Giving – doing things for others, donating our time, ideas and energy. Helping others makes the 'helper' feel good too.

Relating – connecting with other people. People with strong social relationships are happier and healthier.

Exercise – being active increases happiness and improves our mood.

Appreciating – appreciating and taking notice of the world around us helps us to feel better.

Trying out – learning new things helps us to stay curious and engaged, whether through formal learning, hobbies or learning new skills.

Direction – Having goals to look forward to can motivate us and helps us to feel good about the future.

Resilience – 'bouncing back' and how we respond to negative situations has an impact on our wellbeing.

Emotion – experiencing positive emotions such as joy, gratitude, contentment and inspiration improves wellbeing, as does having a positive attitude.

Acceptance – accepting ourselves and not comparing ourselves to others increase feelings of happiness.

Meaning – being part of something bigger and having meaning and purpose in our lives help us to feel happier, more in control and more purposeful.

Even just reading these you may already be identifying some reasons why individuals on the autism spectrum can find it harder to feel a sense of happiness and wellbeing. You will learn more throughout this book about possible challenges for those on the autism spectrum and how to overcome them.

REMEMBER! This is a very brief overview. Look at the 'Further Reading and Resources' section at the end of this book if you are interested in finding out more.

POSITIVE PSYCHOLOGY AS A MAINSTREAM MOVEMENT

Findings from the positive psychology movement are rapidly entering popular culture and mainstream organisations. In fact, barely a day goes by without the popular media containing some mention of how we can improve our happiness or wellbeing. So, where has this interest come from?

Until the end of the twentieth century psychology was focused mainly on remediating diseases and disorders, on getting people back to a 'normal' level of functioning. Psychologists examined medical disorders and a trip to the psychologists would have usually had negative associations – there must be something very 'wrong' with you. However, the last century was a time of huge change in most economically developed countries. Most of us no longer have to worry about having enough food to eat or finding shelter. We have access to education, health and care services. Now that our basic needs have been met the focus of our attention has shifted – we now no longer have to worry about survival, so can think instead about improving our levels of happiness and wellbeing.

In addition, the overt consumerism of the later twentieth century has contributed to changing attitudes. The myth was perpetuated that wealth would bring happiness – that we should strive for a higher income, a large house, cars and other possessions as these would improve our levels of wellbeing. This general view has shifted in recent years, with society having almost reached saturation point when it comes to material possessions. Many are realising that despite this wealth they still feel unhappy inside. The rapid increase in mental health difficulties in society is leading individuals, professionals and large organisations to look for preventative ways of promoting happiness and wellbeing. Positive psychology is not about treating mental illness, but more about helping anybody to increase their happiness, improve their wellbeing and develop positive ways of coping.

THE BENEFITS OF USING POSITIVE PSYCHOLOGY AS AN APPROACH

Just as within the general population, emotional wellbeing and happiness have received little attention in the field of autism studies until recently. Most interventions for autistic individuals instead have considered success criteria to be based on increasing independence and adaptive functioning (e.g. getting a job, needing less support, living independently, having friends or reducing socially 'unacceptable' behaviour). The assumption that these things will also bring happiness and thriving for autistic people needs to be challenged (Vermeulen 2014). It does not follow that an autistic individual who lives independently will automatically be happier, just as it should not be assumed that an individual who needs a high level of support will be unhappy.

Indeed, there is in fact little evidence that improving outcomes such as level of independence or social skills also improves happiness levels in autistic individuals. Some evidence suggests that the 'severity' of a person's autism has far less impact on wellbeing levels than the discrepancy between their needed and received support (Renty and Royers 2006). So, whatever the level of an individual's needs, if they feel they are receiving the necessary support for these, they will be happier than if they feel they are not receiving the support they need. Other studies have indicated that greater perceived support from family and friends is associated with a better quality of life for autistic individuals (Khanna *et al.* 2014) and that quality of life in autistic individuals was found to correlate with taking part in regular and meaningful recreational activities, rather than being related to their occupation, intelligence or housing situation (Billstedt, Gillberg and Gillberg 2011).

So more of a balance is needed when considering the desired outcomes for individuals on the autism spectrum. There is no doubt that traditional measures of success are important – academic achievement can mean greater access to jobs, having a job can increase feelings of confidence and competence and improving social skills can reduce the anxiety and misunderstandings that come with social interaction – however, it should not be assumed that these things will automatically improve happiness and wellbeing.

Individuals on the autism spectrum can also be more likely than others to experience mental health difficulties such as depression and anxiety (Van Heijst and Geurts 2014). Some of the reasons for this are discussed later in this book but it is perhaps inevitable that individuals who experience difficulties with social interaction, and find the world to be a confusing and unpredictable place, will experience feelings of loneliness, isolation, uncertainty and depression. Therefore, it is even more important to help children and teens on the autism spectrum to improve their happiness and wellbeing levels.

Many positive psychology interventions have not yet been trialled or adapted for individuals on the autism spectrum. That's why this book has been written – it is just as important to work with autistic students on their happiness and wellbeing as it is any other student, but there are specific issues to take into account when working with students on the autism spectrum and some approaches designed for non-autistic students may not be helpful to autistic students.

This book adapts some evidence-based positive psychology interventions for autism. Professionals need to be aware of using traditional questionnaires and surveys designed for the neurotypical population with individuals on the autism spectrum as there can be difficulties with interpreting questions literally and with communication. Furthermore, it is also important to remember that what makes neurotypical people happy may not also make autistic people happy.

> We should avoid forcing autistic people into a neurotypical concept of happiness; happiness is a personal and subjective construct and the things that make an autistic person happy do not necessarily mirror those that make a neurotypical person happy. (Vermeulen 2014, p.14)

POSITIVE PSYCHOLOGY? IS THAT JUST THE SAME AS POSITIVE THINKING?

No, positive psychology is not just the same as positive thinking. Having a positive attitude does help, and some aspects of positive psychology do focus on helping individuals and organisations to develop this, but positive psychology is based on scientific evidence as to what has been proven to be helpful. Positive psychology is 'positive' in that it is concerned with developing the positive things in life, such as human strengths, beneficial emotions, wellbeing, resilience and flourishing.

This chapter has not been designed to provide a complete overview of the field of positive psychology, which is now a rapidly expanding area, but instead been designed as a starting point for applying some of the findings of the movement to working with students on the autism spectrum. For more detailed information about specific aspects of positive psychology, follow some of the links in the 'Further Reading and Resources' section of this book.

4

RECOGNISING, IDENTIFYING AND USING CHARACTER STRENGTHS

CHARACTER STRENGTHS: THE THEORY

This chapter looks at character strengths and the benefits of identifying, recognising and utilising these.

YOUR TURN

What are your strengths? Make a list.

How easy did you find it to list your strengths? When I ask groups of adults this question during training sessions, I am often met with groans, uneasy giggles and frowns of concentration as participants struggle to identify what their strengths might be. The problem is certainly not that I am surrounded by people who lack strengths, but rather that, in the United Kingdom at least, many of us seem to be uncomfortable in admitting our more positive qualities! If asked, 'What are your weaknesses?' most people would have no difficulty in assembling a longer and more detailed list! Many of us find it easy to be critical towards ourselves, but more difficult to show ourselves kindness and compassion.

When working with children and young people in school settings, I often encounter slightly different difficulties. Most children can identify subjects that they are good at or activities that they enjoy ('maths', 'history' or 'PE'), but very few can identify any general strengths or positive characteristics that they might have.

KEY TERMS

Strengths, skills, gifts, talents – what is the difference?

Character strengths. Character strengths are generally considered to be positive character traits used across various aspects of our personal, educational, social or vocational lives. Examples of character strengths include creativity, gratitude, perseverance, teamwork or appreciation of beauty.

Skills. A skill is usually considered to be an acquired ability or expertise which has required training or practice. These can be 'hard' skills (such as computer skills, reading, budgeting, gardening) or 'soft' skills which are harder to measure (such as listening skills, friendship skills and communication skills).

Gifted and talented. The term 'gifted and talented' is often used by schools to describe children and young people who have the potential to develop beyond what is usually expected for their age. 'Gifted' refers to pupils who have abilities in academic subjects, while 'talented' is used to refer to children who have abilities in subjects such as art, music or sport. A 'gift' or 'talent' is usually considered to be an innate aptitude for a certain area.

The importance of recognising and using our strengths

The concept of identifying and developing strengths is central to positive psychology. So why is it important to be able to recognise our strengths? Research suggests that there are many links between strengths, wellbeing and life satisfaction:

- Knowing our strengths helps us to gain personal insight and helps us to make better decisions.

- Recognising and following our strengths generates optimism (Boniwell 2008).

- Using our strengths feels authentic and energising (Linley 2008).

- Knowledge of our strengths helps to bring a sense of fulfilment and helps us to achieve our goals (Boniwell 2008; Linley *et al.* 2010).

- Top achievers have been shown to build their lives around their talents and strengths, while recognising, understanding and managing their weaknesses (Clifton and Anderson 2001).

- Adolescents' knowledge and development of their strengths has a positive effect on preventing negative outcomes and indicates positive development and thriving (Park and Peterson 2006).

- People who use their strengths more have higher levels of self-efficacy (Govindji and Linley 2007) and self-esteem (Minhas 2010).

- Putting our strengths to work on a daily basis can have a lasting positive effect on our happiness levels (Boniwell 2015).

- Using our core strengths means we are likely to feel more confident, less stressed and are more likely to achieve our goals (King 2015).

- Further evidence suggests that strengths-based interventions can have lasting effects (Wilson 2011) as young people then develop a more positive view of themselves which can lead to sustained change.

Focusing on strengths does not mean blindly overlooking any weaknesses, as ignoring these could also lead to an unrealistic sense of self. Positive psychology instead advocates working towards strengths and finding new ways to apply these in our lives, while at the same time recognising our lower strengths and using our top strengths to manage and develop these. It is also important to note that in some studies the positive effects of using strengths only endured if participants were told to use a chosen strength in a new and different way each day, rather than if they were just told to use their strengths more (Seligman *et al.* 2005). Therefore it is not only important for young people to be supported to recognise their strengths but also to be taught how to put these to use.

How are strengths classified?

So we know why identifying our strengths is important, but just what exactly counts as a strength?

Strengths have been classified in different ways. Perhaps the best known is the VIA Character Survey which identifies 24 different strengths, split into six different categories. A further classification system, the Gallup's StrengthsFinder, identifies 34 different strengths, and other systems recognise different numbers and types of strengths. Generally, all classification systems consider strengths to be traits which are considered positive across different cultures and societies.

Some commonly identified strengths include:

Adaptability, Appreciation of beauty, Authenticity, Bravery, Creativity, Critical thinking, Curiosity, Emotional intelligence, Enthusiasm, Equality, Fairness, Forgiveness, Generosity, Gratitude, Honesty, Hope, Humour, Integrity, Justice, Kindness, Leadership, Love of learning, Loving, Modesty, Open-mindedness, Optimism, Organisation, Originality, Patience, Perseverance, Perspective, Prudence, Relationships, Responsibility, Self-awareness, Self-control, Social intelligence, Spirituality, Teamwork, Vitality, Wisdom.

YOUR TURN

Make another list of your strengths. Using the words above may help. Can you think of any other strengths to add? Now identify examples of when you use each of your strengths. Can you identify any further opportunities to use your top strengths in your life?

It can often be helpful to ask trusted others what they believe your strengths are. Any sort of self-evaluation brings with it an element of bias, so try to be as honest with yourself as you can.

The strengths that an individual possesses the most are often called their 'signature strengths'. These are the strengths that, when we use and cultivate them, help us to feel authentic and energised. So, for example, somebody who would consider a 'love of learning' as their signature strength is likely to feel vibrant and fulfilled when working in a job which involves gaining new knowledge, when researching a new hobby or when finding out about a new holiday destination. The same person may feel bored and unfulfilled when in a repetitive, monotonous job with no opportunities for new learning. So, knowledge of our strengths can help us to seek out situations which fulfil us, rather than ones which are less meaningful to us.

Now that you have considered your own strengths and thought about why these are important, it is time to consider how you can support young people on the autism spectrum to identify and develop their personal strengths too.

Strengths and individuals on the autism spectrum

We have seen why it can be beneficial for us all to be able to recognise our signature strengths; the awareness improves not only our self-esteem and confidence, but also helps us to reach our goals and make more effective decisions relating to our education, employment, relationships and personal lives. But why is this knowledge particularly important to develop in young people on the autism spectrum?

- Recognising strengths is a good way for students to start to identify their positive qualities and what is good about them, rather than focusing on what is different or difficult. It can also help them to start to realise how other people are different to themselves.

- Research suggests that children and young people on the autism spectrum can have lower self-esteem and self-worth than their more typically developing peers (Jamison and Schuttler 2015). There are several explanations for this: young people on the autism spectrum may experience direct, and indirect, comparisons to their peers; they may receive negative reactions from others; may feel 'odd', 'different' or 'wrong' and may feel that it is not ok to be themselves.

- Some young people on the autism spectrum, perhaps particularly females, can also lack a secure sense of self-identity (Simone 2010). This could be because they try hard to copy or mimic others in order to 'fit in', perhaps try to hide aspects of themselves which they consider to be less acceptable or perhaps have fewer opportunities and interactions with others which allow them to develop a sense of self and individuality.

- Children and young people on the autism spectrum may find that they often end up focusing on their perceived 'weaknesses' or areas they need to improve on. Targets set at school may focus on comparing students with neurotypical expectations, rather than on what they already do well. This emphasis can lead to an unbalanced focus on the 'negatives'.

- Young people on the autism spectrum may have strengths which have never been recognised as such, and therefore perceive them as negatives. Take a young person who has an intense hyperfocus and perseverance on a special interest, for example. Instead of this being recognised as a strength, she might have been told that she is selfish for not participating in family life, or 'odd' for not pursuing more typical leisure pursuits. Equally a young person who quickly identifies inconsistencies and discrepancies may be told that he is being pedantic or facetious, when such an ability would be highly sought after in careers such as the law or academia.

- Evidence also suggests that children and young people on the autism spectrum are more likely to experience mental health difficulties, including depression, anxiety and obsessive-compulsive disorder (Kim *et al.* 2000). Research on the value of knowing and following your strengths indicates that this can generate optimism, confidence and bring a sense of fulfilment (Boniwell 2008) and so can support positive mental wellbeing.

In the autism literature you may come across lists of 'autistic strengths'. These often include characteristics such as:

- specialist knowledge of topics of interest
- excellent memory for facts and figures
- high motivation for special interests
- accuracy
- attention to detail
- following instructions precisely
- seeing the world from a different perspective
- innovative
- honest
- non-judgemental
- sense of loyalty
- unique sense of humour
- logical
- less concern for what others think
- independent
- stick to routines
- enjoy their own company.

Many of these things are strengths for individuals on the autism spectrum but remember not to be limited by such lists – autistic individuals are as varied as their non-autistic counterparts so do not be restricted by stereotypes.

CHARACTER STRENGTHS: PUTTING IT INTO PRACTICE
Group activities

BUILDING UP A STRENGTHS VOCABULARY

(7–11, 11–14, 14–16, 16–18)

Aim: To increase knowledge of vocabulary related to strengths.

Resources: Download and print the 'Strengths and Definitions Cards' from Appendix A. One set of each per small group.

How to do it: Many children and young people will not yet have the vocabulary to describe and explain their strengths. This activity supports children to build up that vocabulary. Explain to the group that you are going to be doing some work today about people's strengths and positive traits.

1. Divide the larger group into pairs or smaller groups. Give each small group or pair both sets of cards. Some students may benefit from being given just a few at a time to make the task easier.

2. Groups are to discuss the cards and try to match the words with their definitions.

3. If students find the activity difficult, suggest that they begin with the ones they already know. Which are left over? Are they able to match any more?

4. Facilitate whole-group feedback, asking students if they can give examples of each strength.

5. Pay particular attention to words or concepts that were new to the group; try to focus on these when working on some of the other activities in this chapter.

STRENGTH OF THE WEEK

(7–11, 11–14, 14–16)

Aim: To encourage a deeper understanding of strengths vocabulary.

Resources: A display board or whiteboard. Sticky notes or small squares of paper.

How to do it: This activity encourages students to link the strengths vocabulary they are learning to their own lives. It could be a suitable activity for circle time, assembly or home-time.

1. Choose a strengths word of the week (e.g. 'Kindness'). Place this word in the centre of the display board. Talk through the word with the group, ensuring that all understand its meaning.

2. Give students the challenge of noticing examples of this strength this week. There may be examples of them using the strength, of others (friends, family, relatives) using the strength, or examples that they see in the media or on the news.

3. When students observe an example, ask them to record this on a sticky note or piece of paper (in words or drawings) and add it to the strengths board. You may encourage students to add to the board whenever an example occurs to them, or alternatively have a set time each day to discuss and add to the board as a group. Examples: Kindness.

   'I saw that there was a new girl at computer club so I asked if she would like to sit next to me and I told her what we had been doing.'

   'I left my pencil case at home but Amid lent me a pen and pencil to use for the day.'

4. During, or at the end of, the week, have a group reflection session to talk through all of the examples that the group has collected. Explain why these examples show the strength being used.

5. Choose a different strengths word for the following week.

FAMOUS PEOPLE AND THEIR STRENGTHS

(7–11, 11–14, 14–16, 16–18)

Aim: To identify how famous people have put their strengths to good use.

Resources: Printed photos and factfiles of famous people or access to the internet; download and print Appendix B.

How to do it:

1. Print out a selection of pictures of famous people relevant to the age group you are working with. Choose a selection of: sportspeople, authors, artists, musicians, entrepreneurs, political or governmental leaders, religious leaders, advocates for different causes, local celebrities. Provide a short factfile of their work and achievements.

2. Provide students with the 'Strengths and Definitions Lists' (Appendix B). Ask students to work in pairs. Give each group a small selection of photos and ask them to identify strengths that they think each famous person demonstrates. Students may also identify further strengths not listed.

3. Older students may like to add their own famous people to the list and use the internet to research these people.

4. Ask each pair to feed back to the larger group. They should introduce the famous person to the group, give a

short biography and explain which strengths they have shown. Example:

'This is J.K. Rowling. She has written the Harry Potter series of books which have been made into popular films. She has also written books for adults, and plays. We think she is very creative, because she thought up the Harry Potter world. We also think she is perseverant as she did not give up after receiving many rejections, and we think she is generous as she has set up her own charity.'

IDEAS OF FAMOUS PEOPLE TO USE

- Arts: J.K. Rowling, Emma Watson, Ed Sheeran, David Walliams, Jamie Oliver, Jacqueline Wilson, Michael Morpurgo

- Business: Richard Branson, Alan Sugar

- Political activists: Martin Luther King, Rosa Parks, Malala, Nelson Mandela

- Sports: Andy Murray, Alistair and Jonathan Brownlee, Mo Farah, Paula Radcliffe, Roger Federer, Bradley Wiggins, Chris Froome, Ellie Simmonds, David Weir

SUPERHERO STRENGTHS

(7–11, 11–14, 14–16)

Aim: To create a superhero and identify his or her strengths.

Resources: Paper and coloured pens and crayons, or computer design software; download and print Appendix B.

How to do it:

1. Ask each student to design a superhero. Show some examples of superheroes to provide ideas and ask students to share details of their favourite superheroes first. Encourage students to be as creative as they like when designing – What does the superhero look like? What does s/he wear? Does s/he have any special gadgets?

2. Ask students to identify their superhero's strengths. Provide the 'Strengths and Definitions List' (Appendix B) for them to refer to. Students can write their superhero's top three strengths on their pictures.

3. Students then present their superhero to the rest of the group. They should show their picture, describe their superhero and explain his or her strengths, giving examples of how they use these. (Example: 'My superhero is very organised – he always takes with him what he might need, his invisibility cloak, his super-fast sneakers and his glasses which allow him to see through walls.')

4. If time allows, ask students to create a story with their superhero as central character. Their story should show their superhero using his or her strengths. Students may like to draw a cartoon strip, make a computer animation or act out the story. Students then share these stories with the rest of the group and discuss the strengths being displayed by the superheroes.

I'M ME, YOU'RE YOU

(7–11, 11–14, 14–16)

Aim: To support students to see how we each have different likes and dislikes; it's normal to be different.

Resources: Pens and paper or other recording devices. Chairs set out in pairs around the room. Some students may benefit from visual prompts such as pictures or symbols.

How to do it: Explain that each one of us is different, we all have different preferences, likes and dislikes. It's normal to be different; life would be very boring if we were all the same! In this activity we are going to get to know other people in the group to find out more about our differences and similarities.

1. Ask students to think of between three and eight questions they would like to ask other people in the group to find out about their preferences, likes and dislikes. The number and type of question you ask students to design will depend on the age and ability of the group. Explain to students that 'open questions' will work better than ones which invite a 'yes/no' answer. Some examples may include:

    - What is your favourite colour?

    - What is your favourite animal?

    - What is your favourite television show?

    - What is your favourite film?

    - What is your favourite food?

    - Which food do you hate?

    - What are your hobbies?

    - Where is your favourite place?

    - What is your favourite subject?

    - What is your favourite sport?

    - Where would be your dream holiday?

2. Once students have made their lists (each student should have a different set of questions, although there may be some overlap), divide students into pairs. Students take

it in turns to ask each other the questions and record the answers they are given (in writing, in pictures, on a tally chart or on a tablet or laptop).

3. After two minutes, ask one of each pair to move on to another student and complete the same task. Every two minutes (or shorter or longer depending on the group), ask students to move on, until they are back to their original partner.

4. This activity can be a good way of encouraging students to speak to others they might not know very well and to identify possible shared interests. It can also help to 'structure' a conversation for students on the autism spectrum who may have difficulty with this. As students are carrying out the task be aware of fostering an atmosphere of acceptance and encourage students to show interest, rather than negativity, towards others' preferences.

5. Feedback for this activity can be taken in a number of ways. You might like to ask students if they found others with shared interests, or if they learned anything new about others from the activity. Some students may like to turn their results into a chart for display. Alternatively, the group may like to create a 'we're all different' display. Perhaps create different areas on the display board (e.g. 'Our favourite foods', 'Our favourite animals', 'Our religions') and ask students to put a picture or drawing of their preferences on each one.

OUR OWN STRENGTHS

(11–14, 14–16, 16–18)

Aim: For students to begin to identify their own top strengths.

Resources: Download and print Appendix B.

How to do it: This activity works best when students are familiar with the strengths vocabulary after completing some of the previous activities.

1. Give each student a copy of Appendix B, the 'Strengths and Definitions List'.

2. Ask each student to highlight what they think their top three to five strengths are. Reinforce the fact that there are no right or wrong answers; everybody should have a different list.

3. Ask students to think of examples when they have used these strengths. Students can make notes or do a small drawing next to the strengths they have highlighted.

4. Sometimes it can be difficult to recognise our own strengths. Ask students to approach two or three other people in the group and tell them what strengths they have noticed. The adults in the room can also join in and suggest to some students any strengths they have noticed.

5. Armed with this knowledge, ask students to create a small poster, or computer presentation, of their top strengths. They can illustrate this with examples of when they have demonstrated these strengths.

USING TOP STRENGTHS TO DEVELOP LOWER STRENGTHS

(11–14, 14–16, 16–18)

Aim: To support students to recognise that they have top strengths and lesser strengths. They can use their top strengths to help to develop their lesser strengths.

Resources: Download and print Appendix B; any activities already completed from this chapter; sticky notes; A3 paper.

How to do it:

1. Place students with a supportive peer, or in small groups.

2. Using the knowledge gained from previous activities, ask students to each write their top three strengths on sticky notes. They should discuss with their partner why they believe they possess each strength and any examples they have of them using it.

3. Now each student is to identify one strength from Appendix B they would consider to be one of their lower strengths; an area they would like to improve at or develop. They should share this with their partner and write the strength on a different coloured sticky note and put it in the centre of their piece of paper.

4. Next students work with their partner to identify as many ways as possible that they could use their top strengths to develop their lesser strength. As a pair they can write or draw these ideas on the paper in the form of a spider diagram. Tell students they should not worry at this point about which ideas are most realistic, but just to record all of their ideas and thoughts. Students then swap around, and do the same for the other student in the group.

5. Finally, ask students to look at their spider diagrams and identify one idea that they would like to try. Ask them to be as specific as possible in what they will do. These examples may help:

   'I think patience is one of my lesser strengths as I often get impatient when I am waiting or have nothing to do. However, one of my top strengths is organisation, so I am going to try planning in advance. I will always put a book or my headphones in my bag so that when

I am out and feel I am getting impatient, I will have something to do to stop me feeling so frustrated.'

'Teamwork is one of my lesser strengths at the moment, but some of my top strengths are following instructions and reliability. So next time there is a team task I will volunteer to be the note-taker and I will tick off each step as we do it. I will tell the rest of the team what we have to do next and how much time we have left to do it.'

TOP TIP! It is not necessary to be too concerned about the difference between skills and strengths at this point; indeed there is some overlap. What is more important is that children and young people begin to build a picture about the positive strengths and skills that they possess. If a student finds it easier to identify skills rather than strengths, help them to prise out the strengths they have used to develop those skills. So, for example, a child who recognises that they have good computer skills may have read lots of books about computers to find out more, or may not have always been so good at computers but kept on practising until they became more proficient – these could link to strengths of perseverance or determination. Try to support students to move away from ideas such as 'I'm good at maths' or 'I'm good at football' and recognise more general strengths which can be transferred across situations. If students build their self-esteem solely on being good at maths, football and so on, they might find that this is easily shattered when they move to another class or team, or when somebody more talented comes along!

SKILLS AND STRENGTHS SWAP

(7–11, 11–14, 14–16, 16–18)

Aim: To support students to recognise their own skills and strengths and those of others. To help students to use their strengths and skills to support others.

Resources: List of skills (below), resources depending on the skills chosen.

LIST OF POSSIBLE 'SKILLS' TO CHOOSE FROM

Being punctual, handing in homework on time, drawing, painting, origami, organisation, doing homework, reading, giving presentations to the class, working in a group, making videos, creating a presentation, touch typing, designing apps and games, playing chess or draughts, playing dominoes (or any other traditional game, card game or board game), presenting work neatly, playing a musical instrument, dancing, singing, reading music, making an animation, sewing, juggling, looking after animals, playing with younger children, learning another language, working independently.

Students can also add their own to this list.

How to do it:

1. Students first need to identify their top three skills. These may be linked to their top strengths which they will have already identified if they have completed previous activities in this chapter. However, for this activity, skills rather than strengths may work better, particularly with younger students. Provide a list of skills, such as the one above, and ask students to choose their top three. Students next need to choose three skills they would like to develop further. The list may need to be modified depending on the age of the students, and students should be encouraged to

add other 'skills' they feel they possess or would like to improve if they are not already on the list.

2. Students then need to be partnered up with other students. This may work best if adults collect in the lists of skills and cross-reference them. Each student needs another student with whom to 'swap' one of their skills. So, for example, a student who had chosen 'drawing' as their top skill may be placed with a student who had chosen drawing as a skill they would like to develop.

3. Once students have been allocated a partner to whom they are going to 'teach' a skill, and a partner from whom they are going to 'learn' a skill, they then need to be given time to prepare for their 'teaching'. This may be time to collect and bring any resources needed, or time to reflect on the skill (e.g. what habits do they have that mean they are 'punctual' or mean that they get all their homework handed in on time?).

4. Students then take part in the 'skill swap' session with their partner. Spend a set amount of time (around 30 minutes can work well) for one partner to share their skill with the other. Reinforce that the student 'learning' the skills should be encouraged to ask questions. These sessions often work well if there are opportunities for practical activities, so, for example, students showing each other how to play games, draw pictures or make a revision timetable.

5. In the next session, roles are reversed. Students who were 'learning' are now 'teaching'; this may or may not be with the same partner, depending on which skills students wanted to swap.

6. This activity can be done several times, depending on the number of students in the group and the skills they have

to share. The activity can be a good way for students to recognise and share their skills with others.

Individual activities

WHAT ARE MY STRENGTHS?

(11–14, 14–16, 16–18)

Aim: For students to begin to identify their individual strengths.

Resources: Download and print the 'Strengths and Definitions Cards' from Appendix A.

How to do it:

1. Provide Appendix A as two sets of cards. Ask the student to match the words with the definitions. Are any words new to the student? Teach the meanings of these words using examples relevant to the student's own life.

2. Ask the student to identify their top strengths (two to five strengths usually works well). Can they give examples of when they have used these strengths? They could discuss these or draw them depending on their preference.

3. If the student has difficulty doing this, ask instead for them to identify things that they have done well in the past. What achievements are they proud of? What do they enjoy doing? What is the favourite part of their week? When have they overcome a problem or fear? What have they got better at? Perhaps record these in a spider diagram. Use these to help the student to identify their strengths. Example:

   - If a student enjoys going to gardening club then perhaps one of their strengths is a love of nature? If they enjoy working by themselves in the garden, then perhaps they are independent? Have they used recycled materials to build the fence? Then perhaps they are environmentally aware. Have they looked after the vegetable patch? Then perhaps they are responsible and reliable.

4. Once the student has identified their top strengths, help them to identify further opportunities to put these into practice. Example:

   • A student who is environmentally aware may be given a responsibility related to recycling at school or at home. They might also be supported to join an extracurricular nature club.

COLLECTING STRENGTHS

(7–11, 11–14, 14–16, 16–18)

Aim: For students to become aware of the strengths they are using on a daily basis.

Resources: Download and print Appendix B.

How to do it: This activity encourages students to identify strengths that they may have not initially considered themselves to have, and encourages them to recognise the strengths that they are using on a daily basis. This activity works best once students are familiar with the strengths vocabulary, so perhaps begin with some of the activities listed above.

1. Give the student a copy of Appendix B, or another list of strengths. Ensure that they are familiar with all of the words included. For the next week they are going to note each time that they use a strength.

2. Some older students may like to do this independently each evening, others may like to complete it with a parent, or some may benefit from completing it with a member of staff at some point during the school day. Ask students to think back over the past 24 hours and to look at the list of

strengths. Which have they used? Make brief notes as a memory aid. Example: Wednesday:

- Resourcefulness: 'I was by myself at lunchtime so I decided to go to homework club to get some work done instead of standing by myself.'

- Gratitude: 'I was grateful because Dad made me my favourite meal as a surprise!'

- Enthusiasm: 'I was very enthusiastic about going to trampoline club after school and I put a lot of effort into it.'

3. At the end of the week reflect with the student on their strengths diary. Which strengths have they been using over the week? Can you help them to identify any others?

STRENGTHS SURVEYS

(11–14, 14–16, 16–18)

Aim: For students to identify their top strengths.

Resources: Computer or mobile device with internet connection.

How to do it: This is another way of supporting children and young people to identify their strengths by using an online survey.

1. Students complete the online survey for 10–17-year-olds at www.viacharacter.org (free of charge at time of writing). Students will need to register an email address, so ensure that they have parental permission.

2. Support the student to work through the survey, explaining what the questions mean if required. Encourage students to be as honest as they can be, answering how they think they are, not how they think they should be or would like to be.

3. Talk through the results with the student. Do they agree with the top strengths that have been identified? If so, can they think of times when they have demonstrated these strengths? Can they identify any other opportunities when they can put these strengths to use?

DEVELOPING LOWER STRENGTHS

(11–14, 14–16, 16–18)

Aim: For students to identify lesser strengths which they would like to develop.

Resources: Download and print Appendix B.

How to do it: This activity invites students to identify lesser strengths, or areas they would like to develop. The emphasis is on developing the attitude that students are able to improve areas that they would like to, building a growth mindset and confidence.

1. Ask the student to look at the list of strengths. Is there a strength listed which they think they would like to develop?

2. Once the student has identified an area they would like to develop, ask them to rate themselves on a scale of 0–10 for this strength. Why have they placed themselves at that point? What are they already doing well? What would they be doing differently to get a higher score?

3. Now ask the student to identify one thing that they could do to move up one step on the scale. Encourage them to be as specific as possible and to identify small, achievable steps. Example:

> 'I have given myself a "1" for organisation as I forget equipment and forget my homework. To move up to "2" I could set an alarm on my mobile phone to go

off at 8.30 every evening. When I hear it I will pack my schoolbag for the next day, putting in everything I need.'

4. The student is to put this idea into place over the next week and monitor their progress. Reflect with the student at the end of the week. What went well? Is there anything that the student is going to continue to do? Does the student need to do something differently? Draw attention to the fact that the student is capable of making positive changes.

5. This activity can then be done at a later date, with a different strength, or with the same strength, identifying how to move even further up the scale.

TOP TIP! Individuals on the autism spectrum interpret the world around them and relate to others in a different way to other people. It is not a 'wrong' way of viewing the world, just perhaps different to the majority or to what is usually expected. Some students may argue that some of the strengths listed are not always strengths, or are not important to them. That is fine; it is a good opportunity to highlight how everybody can have different opinions, but that they are all equally valid.

ACCEPTANCE

(7–11, 11–14, 14–16, 16–18)

Aim: For students to reflect on who they are and to build up a positive self-image.

Resources: Drawing and craft materials or computer software, depending on the student's preference.

How to do it: Some students on the autism spectrum may prefer to work on this project independently before sharing it with an adult. Many will benefit from completing this over a longer period of time as it can be difficult to think of examples 'on the spot'.

1. Explain to the student how this is a small project to help them to identify their individuality. Give the student the following prompts:

   - I'm good at…

   - My strengths are…

   - I'm getting better at…

   - I'd like to get better at…

   - What is most important to me is…

   - My greatest achievement so far is…

   - I like being me because…

   - Others like me because…

   - My dreams for the future include…

   - I feel happiest when…

   - My favourite things are…

   - Advantages of my autism are…

2. Decide how the student would like to prepare this piece of work – perhaps they want to write or type answers, create a spider diagram, make a collage or poster, use computer software, make a model or just talk through their answers. Give students time to reflect on the questions – perhaps they wish to consult scrapbooks, yearbooks or photo albums for ideas or to ask trusted friends or family members why they like the student.

3. Discussion of this project should be a positive and supportive experience. Ask the student to tell you about each of their answers and help them to identify future opportunities for developing some of these areas.

WHAT AUTISM MEANS TO ME

Aim: For students to reflect on how they feel autism affects them and to gain a deeper insight and acceptance of their differences.

Resources: Books, videos, leaflets (depending on the individual).

How to do it:

1. Divide a large sheet of paper into three sections. Label the first 'What I already know'. Ask the student to identify what they already know about autism and how it affects them. Students may be at different stages of awareness; some may have a detailed insight, others may know very little. Discussing the student's answers can be a good opportunity to dispel any myths or misconceptions they might have.

2. Label the second column 'What I would like to know'. Ask the student to identify as many questions as they like about their autism. Students often ask questions such as 'Will I be able to get a job?' 'Will I be able to have a relationship?' 'Will I always have autism?' 'How am I different to others?' 'Why do I feel...?' 'Is...related to my autism?'

3. Next comes the research. There are many books available which explain autism to children and teenagers, there are also leaflets available from local autism organisations. There are also useful videos available and informative websites (such as the National Autistic Society). Ensure that any information you do present is reliable and age appropriate. Some students may learn better from speaking to an older student or young adult on the autism spectrum.

4. Once the previous stage has been complete (it may take a number of sessions to gather answers), label the third section of the paper 'What I have learned'. Ask the student

to identify everything they have learned about their autism from their research. This can be a useful visual reminder of the new knowledge they have gained.

Adult communication

Use a strengths vocabulary

Many children and young people on the autism spectrum may not have the vocabulary with which to describe their own, or other people's, strengths. Support them by using this vocabulary in your own talking. Point out examples of people using these strengths (in real life, in the media, or even fictional characters) and explain what the words mean. Examples:

- 'In the book, Charlie is very optimistic. He believes everything will turn out well.'

- 'The author must be very perseverant and resilient. She submitted her story to many publishers and received many rejections, but she kept trying and did not give up.'

As with anything, do not go overboard with this, just try to notice when there are opportunities to explain strengths in everyday conversation.

Draw attention to students' strengths

Help children and young people to recognise the strengths that they are using in everyday life. Draw attention to what they have done and why this is positive. Examples:

- 'India and Ameera, I think it was great how you split the work equally between you both and asked each other for feedback. That showed real teamwork.'

- 'Joe, you asked the museum curator really interesting questions about the exhibits; it shows you have a real curiosity and interest in the past.'

- 'Ellis, it was very generous of you to spend your break time helping Jacob to look for his coat, thank you.'

- 'Connor, you are very worried as you have forgotten your homework. That's ok, it shows that you are a very responsible person.'

Identify opportunities for students to use their strengths to solve problems

Children and young people on the autism spectrum will encounter difficulties or problems, perhaps on a daily basis. It can be useful to help them to identify how they can use their top strengths to overcome any lesser strengths. Support them to recognise how they can deploy their strengths in different situations. As students become older, support them to try and identify their strengths and how they can solve problems more independently. Examples:

- 'Ben, you said you are bored at lunchtimes and want to do something more interesting. You are very good at researching – maybe you could go onto the school website and see if you can find a list of lunchtime clubs? Then we could see if any would be interesting for you.'

- 'Emily, you are feeling very anxious because you have forgotten to bring your ingredients for cooking this afternoon and you are worried that you will get into trouble. You are a very honest person so perhaps you could go and tell your teacher now that you have realised you left your ingredients on the table at home. She will admire your honesty and will be able to help you find a solution.'

Promote acceptance of difference

As an adult you are in a position to influence the attitudes and perceptions of the young people you work with. Modelling an attitude of acceptance can be hugely beneficial. Cultivate an 'it's ok to be different' atmosphere in your environment. Try not to let any personal prejudices come across and intervene if you do hear young people expressing negative attitudes. A simple statement, delivered in a calm manner, such as 'Everybody is different, some people like playing with others, some prefer to play alone. It's just the way it is. Life would be very boring if we were all exactly the same,' can help children to be more accepting.

Take care with autism awareness

Think carefully about any autism awareness activities which may take place in your setting. Raising awareness of autism amongst staff and students can be a positive way of promoting acceptance and diversity but remember to think carefully about how you will approach this. Consider which materials you will use and the impact that these will have on autistic students (or staff) in your settings. Raising awareness can be very positive if done well, but can increase problems if not planned out well – individuals on the autism spectrum may feel even more different or may not relate to the image that others have been given of autism. If showing videos, giving out printed information or giving a talk or a workshop, consider the language you use and how you present autism – as a disability, disorder, or difference? Are you demonstrating any positives or just negatives? Are you explaining the range of individuals on the autism spectrum? There can be a big difference between a non-verbal person on the autism spectrum with associated learning difficulties, and an individual with Asperger Syndrome. It is best to include students and staff on the autism spectrum in your planning and delivery – are they happy with what you are going to present to their peers? Remember too that 'autism awareness' may inadvertently stigmatise further; there are likely to be students with a range of difficulties and differences in most settings so raising awareness of all of these differences may be more inclusive.

5

CULTIVATING POSITIVE EMOTIONS

The sections in this chapter investigate positive emotions and how these can be increased in children and young people on the autism spectrum. It is important to note that emotions cannot be simply separated into 'positive' and 'negative' and nor should they be presented to children as such. There are no 'right' or 'wrong' emotions. Indeed, experiencing fear, anger, frustration, boredom and worry can all be helpful emotions at times and the aim is not to avoid or eliminate negative emotions but rather to recognise them and respond in more helpful ways. Take a student who is worried about an upcoming exam, for example. This worry could be positive; it may encourage her to focus on preparation and revision. If she was not worried, she might approach the exam without doing any sort of preparation and therefore not do as well as she had hoped. If, however, the worry becomes overwhelming, she might spend so much time caught up in worrying thoughts that she might not be able to do any productive revision at all. So it is not emotions themselves that can be negative, but more our response to them.

That said, there are generally some emotions which are usually considered more 'positive' to experience. These include excitement, joy, interest, satisfaction, contentment, fulfilment, gratitude, calm, zest, pleasure, hope, faith, humour and trust, to name just a few. It can be helpful to promote them in young people as cultivating these emotions can bring many benefits and increase satisfaction with life. Barbara Fredrickson's 'broaden and build' theory (2001) shows how experiencing positive emotions leads to an upwards spiral of more positive emotions, opportunities for personal growth, and further positive emotions. In contrast, negative emotions narrow our focus, thoughts and behaviours. There is also evidence that experiencing positive emotions can act as a 're-set button' (Fredrickson *et al.* 2000), taking us back closer to our original state of being and helping to reduce the impact of the more 'negative' emotion. 'Re-set buttons' could include doing something physical (exercise, walking, gardening), making a connection with something or somebody you care for (people, pets, charity work), doing something to make your body feel calmer (having a bath, massage, relaxation, meditation), doing an activity that takes your mind off things (cooking, cleaning, singing, reading, crosswords), or thinking about things differently (accepting the situation, reframing the situation, journaling, counting blessings) (LeBon 2014).

We first look at how to cultivate positive emotions of happiness and inspiration, flow, hope, optimism and gratitude, before turning our focus in Chapter 6 to developing resilience and a growth mindset to cultivate more helpful responses to less helpful thoughts and emotions.

HAPPINESS, JOY AND INSPIRATION

The concept of personal happiness has gained importance and attention in the past decades. Now that the majority of people in economically developed countries have their basic needs met (food, water, medical supplies, housing, education), their attention has shifted beyond what is needed for survival, and to looking at what can improve their happiness and sense of wellbeing.

Happiness is important to all of us, adults and children. 'Happy' is often one of the first feelings words that many children will learn how to use, and many parents, when talking about their children, will make statements such as, 'I just want him to be happy', or 'I don't mind what she does as long as it makes her happy.' So being happy is important to all of us, but just what does it mean?

> **YOUR TURN**
>
> How would you define happiness? What does happiness mean to you? What makes you happy?

'Happy' is a word we use often but one that is notoriously difficult to define. What makes one person happy may make another person very unhappy! Happiness may mean different things to different people at different times. What did you include in your answer? Perhaps you noted positive feelings and experiences (being with family, laughing with friends, eating chocolate...), or perhaps you considered happiness on a wider scale (being satisfied with your life, generally feeling positive...). Researchers have found that the most commonly cited answers to the 'What makes you happy?' question are relationships, health, contentment, security, personal achievements and concerns for others (Boniwell and Ryan 2012).

The Greek philosopher Aristotle believed that there were two components of happiness:

1. Feeling good (short term) – having fun, enjoying life, having positive relationships, feeling healthy, experiencing pleasure, positive feelings and positive self-talk.

2. Flourishing (longer term) – the result of living a good and meaningful life. Having goals, making a difference to others, feeling you are leading a purposeful and meaningful life.

Aristotle believed that simply 'feeling good' is not enough for happiness, but that true happiness only comes when individuals feel they are living a good life on a wider scale. Research also shows that while pursuing pleasurable activities may increase short-term happiness, pursuing personal growth and greater meaning is more likely to increase long-term happiness. The positive psychology movement also considers these various 'layers' of happiness. Martin Seligman (2002), one of the leading experts in the positive psychology movement, recognised three aspects of happiness:

the pleasant life (the pursuit of positive emotions); the good life (using one's strengths, experiencing flow) and the meaningful life (using one's strengths in service of something greater than yourself).

KEY TERMS

Subjective wellbeing. A term often used in the research literature instead of 'happiness'. Using this term helps to overcome some of the vagueness and ambiguity associated with the word 'happiness'. Happiness can mean different things to different people and can refer to an ongoing state of wellbeing, or a one-off pleasurable activity. Measuring 'happiness' often also relies on using self-evaluations, hence the term 'subjective'.

Flourishing. In his 2011 book, *Flourish*, Martin Seligman explains how he now considers the term 'happiness' to be overused and almost meaningless. He prefers to use the term 'flourishing' to encompass the value more accurately; flourishing comes from gaining meaning and purpose in our lives, experiencing personal growth and feeling part of something bigger than ourselves.

The benefits of happiness and flourishing

It may seem obvious that happiness is a good thing so something that we should strive for. But what does the positive psychology research tell us about the importance of happiness?

- A body of research by Barbara Fredrickson (2009) shows that happier students learn and perform better in the classroom than unhappier students. Happier students tend to be more creative, focused, persistent and energetic.

- Happy people tend to work harder and are more likely to succeed. Happier children have even been found to earn higher salaries when they are adults (Judge and Hurst 2007).

- Happy people have better friends and relationships. They also trust people more and help others more (Boniwell and Ryan 2012).

- Happy people tend to be more creative and show divergent thinking. They are also more likely to persist longer at less enjoyable tasks, and are more systematic and attentive (Lyubomirsky, King and Diener 2005).

- Happiness has also been linked with living a longer life (Danner, Snowdon and Friedsen 2001).

Happiness and autism

Although autistic individuals experience the same range of positive emotions as any other person (although there may be differences in how these are expressed or understood), the evidence indicates that young people on the autism spectrum may be more likely than their neurotypical peers to experience feelings of unhappiness, depression and worry (Van Heijst and Geurts 2014). The exact reasons will differ from individual to individual, but some likely reasons for this include:

- difficulties making and maintaining friendships

- feeling 'different' or 'odd' and not fitting in

- low self-esteem and self-worth

- feeling misunderstood by both adults and peers

- difficulties communicating

- difficulties in understanding and expressing emotions

- school-related difficulties

- finding themselves 'in trouble' for reasons that they do not understand

- frequent misunderstandings

- being more vulnerable to bullying

- anxiety because of sensory overload

- difficulties forming relationships with family members

- increased anxiety about everyday events, particularly if there are

changes to routines or inconsistent rules

- not having difficulties or differences recognised (perhaps particularly in the case of girls on the autism spectrum)

- not understanding why they are 'different'.

Unfortunately mental health problems amongst young people in general are on the rise and it should not be forgotten that all of the issues that affect neurotypical students, can also affect autistic students, who may also find some of these issues even more difficult to navigate than their peers.

- puberty

- sex and relationships

- increasing independence from family members

- social media

- body image

- peer pressure

- school-related pressures

- creating a sense of self-identity

- family difficulties

- career and employment choices.

Research also indicates that negative comparisons and inequality increase unhappiness. So, for example, a disadvantaged child growing up in a disadvantaged area is likely, in fact, to be happier than the same child growing up surrounded by more advantaged children. Internal comparisons can also affect our levels of happiness. If the life we are living is close to our ideal or how we think we 'should' live, then we are likely to be happier than if there is a substantial discrepancy between our present conditions and our 'ideal' vision (Boniwell 2008). Our 'ideal' is likely to be influenced by the media, our family, culture and the society in which we are brought up. Relating this to autism, is it easy to see why some autistic individuals may be less happy than their peers. For young people in many developed countries, the 'ideal' image given by the media is that of having a large friendship group, a best friend (BFF), an intimate relationship, enjoying popular culture and adhering to a certain 'look' or 'style'. For less typical young people, it can be difficult to feel happy in their own skin, if they are constantly being told that they 'should' be a certain way to be happier and more successful.

So it can be important to support young people on the autism spectrum to identify what makes them happy as an individual, not what they think *should* make them happy. Remember also to take into consideration that what makes an autistic person happy may not be what makes a non-autistic person happy; it is important to avoid forcing autistic people into a neurotypical concept of happiness (Vermeulen 2016). Equally, what makes one autistic person happy may not be what makes another autistic person happy! I am autistic and am probably happiest when alone and when engaged in reading or studying maps – there are plenty of other autistic people who would find this very boring indeed and plenty of neurotypical people who would also gain pleasure from these pursuits!

> **TOP TIP!** Try not to encourage students to focus too much on 'being happy' as an outcome. The more that people worry about being happy, the less happy they become!

HAPPINESS, JOY AND INSPIRATION: PUTTING IT INTO PRACTICE

Many of the activities here focus on personal happiness and pursuing enjoyable, pleasurable activities. For activities on how to utilise character strengths to increase happiness see 'Character strengths: Putting it into practice' in Chapter 4, and for activities to promote wider meaning and purpose see 'Meaning and purpose: Putting it into practice' in Chapter 6.

Group activities

HAPPY MEMORIES WALL

(7–11, 11–14)

Aim: For students to reflect on happy memories.

Resources: Display board; photographs; art materials.

How to do it:

1. Ask each student to think of some of their happiest memories. These could be activities, one-off events, people, places, pets, hobbies, feelings, or anything else that comes to mind. Ask students to create a small poster – they might like to add photographs, make a collage, draw, write or present their memories in any other means.

2. Place the posters on to the 'Happy Memories Wall'. Discuss with the class that different things make different people happy.

3. Some students may like to talk about some of their happy memories in more detail to the rest of the class.

4. Students may like to add more memories to the wall throughout the year.

5. Students' 'happy memory posters' can act as a starting point for individual discussion. What has made them happy in the past? Are there opportunities to do more of these things?

> **TOP TIP!** Positive reminiscence, or engaging with fulfilling memories, is seen to be a significant factor for wellbeing in life (Boniwell and Ryan 2012). Other evidence also suggests that positive reminiscence can help to maintain a sense of identity as children grow and mature (Lyubomirsky 2007).

THE HAPPINESS SURVEY

(7–11, 11–14, 14–16)

Aim: To identify that happiness means different things to different people.

Resources: Download and print Appendix C; recording devices (optional).

How to do it:

1. Give each student a copy of Appendix C. Appendix C is a list of things that could be said to create happiness. Talk through the list with the group to ensure that all students understand what each item means.

2. Students are to walk around the classroom asking other students (and adults) which three items on the list make them happiest. Students keep a tally chart of answers. There are blank spaces at the bottom to add other answers.

3. Bring the group back together. Some groups at this point may be able to transform their results into a bar chart, pie chart or other visual representation, using paper or computer software.

4. Discuss the answers obtained. Emphasise that there are no right answers but that happiness means different things to different people.

WHAT IS HAPPINESS?

(11–14, 14–16, 16–18)

Aim: To consider what happiness means.

Resources: Download and print the 'Happiness Statements' from Appendix D and cut into small cards; sticky notes.

How to do it:

1. Divide the class up into smaller groups or pairs.

2. Ask each group to define 'happiness'. What does happiness mean to them? Give the groups a few minutes to discuss this, and to write their thoughts onto sticky notes which they then bring to stick on the board.

3. Pick a few of the sticky notes to share with the class. Comment on the range of different opinions and how 'happiness' means different things to different people. There are no right or wrong answers.

4. Next give each group or pair between one and three cards containing the statements below. Ask them to discuss these for a few moments. Do they agree or disagree? What are the arguments for and against? Can they come to any conclusions?

5. Each small group is now to join another small group to make a slightly larger group and expand the discussion. Are there any differences in option?

6. Now ask each of the original groups to feed back to the class. They should read aloud the statement they were given and summarise their thoughts on the matter. Remember to reiterate that there are no right or wrong answers.

THE SILENT HAPPINESS DEBATE

(14–16, 16–18)

Aim: For older students to consider in more detail what is meant by happiness.

Resources: Download and print the 'Happiness Statements' from Appendix D; large paper; felt pens.

How to do it: This activity can be delivered in different ways, depending on the age and strengths of the students in the group. Some students may enjoy this type of 'silent debate', but others may prefer a traditional oral debate with a partner or even in front of the class.

1. Divide students into groups of four. Give each small group of students one of the statements from the activity above. Explain that they are going to prepare a debate with two people having to agree with the statement and the other two disagreeing. Explain that it does not particularly matter what their personal opinions are, it is about taking on a role.

2. Give students time to research and think about their side of the argument. They might like to make notes, research using the internet, ask other people in the class or ask people at home for a homework task.

3. Once students feel prepared, give each pair a large piece of paper and some felt pens. One student begins by writing a sentence arguing their point, the other pair has to respond in writing. Students take it in turns debating in this 'silent' way. Show students how they can draw arrows to refer to previous points, they may include emoticons to reinforce their points, or even quick drawings. They may respond with questions for their debating 'opponents' to answer.

4. Once students come to the end of these 'silent' debates ask them to look back at their large sheet of paper and discuss their debate. Choose one person from each small group to summarise the main points that came up and feed back to the whole class.

Individual activities

CREATE A YEARBOOK

(7–11, 11–14, 14–16, 16–18)

Aim: To create a working 'yearbook' to highlight and reflect on happy memories, achievements and positive experiences.

Resources: A scrapbook, sketch pad or notebook; photographs; crafting materials.

How to do it:

1. Provide the student with a scrapbook or sketchbook which is going to be their personal 'yearbook'.

2. Set aside times during the term for the student to update their book with happy memories, positive experiences or any other achievements. They might include photographs, drawings, captions, writing, or use any other creative means that they like.

3. Discuss the entries with the students. What is important to them about those memories? What did they enjoy? What did they learn? What made them feel good? What would they like to do more of?

WHAT MAKES ME HAPPY?

(7–11, 11–14, 14–16, 16–18)

Aim: For individuals to explore what helps them to feel happy.

Resources: Art and craft materials; old magazines or photos from the internet.

How to do it:

1. Provide the student with a large piece of paper. Write the following two sentences in the centre: What things make you happy? What does happiness mean to you?

2. Ask the student to create a 'happiness mindmap' to answer the questions. They can write words, draw pictures, stick down photos, make a collage or create something using computer software. Encourage students to be as creative and as original as they like, reiterating that there is no 'right' way of doing this activity.

3. Once finished, discuss the piece with the student. What things have they identified as making them happy? People, animals, objects, places, hobbies? Do the pictures they have chosen suggest particular themes (e.g. nature, animals, quiet, friends)? Help the student to identify what is important to them and why. Discuss whether there are any more opportunities to do the things that they have identified.

HAPPINESS RE-SET BUTTONS

(7–11, 11–14, 14–16, 16–18)

Aim: To identify what students can do to 're-set' their happiness levels at times when they are feeling less comfortable.

Resources: Small cards (see below).

How to do it:

1. Explain to the student that there are different things we can do to help ourselves feel happier when we are feeling tired, bored, frustrated or angry. It can be useful to know what works for us as individuals so that we can put these ideas into practice.

2. Write the following on small cards: exercise, sleep, dancing, music, writing down feelings, bouncing on a trampoline, hitting a punchbag, drawing, laughing, doing crafts, walking, swimming, yoga, talking to a trusted person, having a power nap, relaxation exercises, baking, doing puzzles, reading. Explain how each of these can help us to feel calmer and can improve our wellbeing (see 'Wellbeing' in Chapter 6 for details on how each of these things can help if needed).

3. Ask the student to identify times when they feel unhappy, frustrated, angry or annoyed. What do they usually do and does this help? Could they try one of the new ideas from the cards? Examples:

   - Joe feels bored and unhappy when he gets home from school because his computer is broken and he has nothing to do. He gets frustrated at his younger siblings who he thinks 'wind him up'. He ends up going to his bedroom and crying. The whole evening is ruined for him. He likes Pokemon so next time he is going to draw his Pokemon characters when he goes to his room and see how this makes him feel.

   - Ellie feels angry when she gets home from school because she remembers all of the things that have irritated her during the day. She can't stop thinking about them and by the time she goes to bed they have become major problems. Tonight she will try bouncing on her trampoline in the garden for a while and then taking the dog for a walk with her mum. She will see if the exercise helps her to feel calmer.

4. Help the student to arrange the resources they need to try out this method when the time next occurs (e.g. a notebook, a funny video link). Ask them to feed back to you whether the activity had a positive impact on their mood.

TOP TIP! Children and young people on the autism spectrum may also experience sensory discomfort or overload, which can lead to 'shutdown' or 'meltdown' if not avoided. You can also use this activity to help them to identify what to do to help them cope with sensory over-stimulation. Possible solutions might be to find a quiet space, be alone for a while, take a power nap, or to use coping strategies such as ear plugs or tinted glasses.

Adult communication
Avoid comparisons

Being compared to others, or being compared indirectly to an 'ideal', will reduce happiness, especially for young people on the autism spectrum who can interpret things very literally. Avoid using the word 'should' as this can lead to young people on the autism spectrum believing that their thoughts or feelings are 'wrong' or unacceptable. Statements such as 'Young people like you should love going outside with your friends' can make the individual feel that there is something 'wrong' with them if this is not something that they enjoy.

Help to create happy memories

Get into the habit of 'collecting' happy memories for the students you work with. Take photos or short videos of them enjoying positive experiences. Collect memorabilia such as tickets or leaflets.

Use these to create scrapbooks, photo albums, yearbooks or displays with the children and young people you work with. This can be a good opportunity to relive and discuss these happy memories.

End on a positive

Studies show that our emotional memories depend on how an experience ends (Rae and MacConville 2015). Therefore, support students by concluding activities, events, lessons and the school day with a focus on the positives and what has gone well.

HOPE AND OPTIMISM

In this section, we explore how being hopeful and optimistic can improve wellbeing. We look at how we can increase hopeful and optimistic thinking in the students we work with.

YOUR TURN

Would you consider yourself an optimist or a pessimist? Are you generally hopeful or unhopeful about the future? What do you think are the benefits of a hopeful attitude?

Being hopeful reflects a positive expectation about something happening in the future and this helps people to stay healthy, to improve performance and to cope with difficulties in life. It is thought that being hopeful:

- helps to reduce self-critical thoughts

- increases focus on the positives

- enables people to create a mental plan

- increases focus and motivation

- helps us to achieve goals

- contributes to our feelings of happiness and wellbeing.

Hopeful adults focus on success rather than failure, experience fewer negative feelings when encountering obstacles and are more able to break down large, vague tasks into small, manageable problems (Snyder 2000).

KEY TERMS

Optimists. Optimists have a sense of confidence about the future. They generally expect outcomes to be positive.

Pessimists. Pessimists generally expect outcomes to be negative. They have a sense of doubt and hesitancy.

Positive psychology research has found many advantages to optimistic thinking (Boniwell 2008). Optimists tend to be able to deal with difficulties more positively, adapt better to negative events, learn lessons from negatives, are less likely to give up, engage more in health-promoting behaviours and seem more productive in the workplace.

TOP TIP! Being hopeful is not just about wishful thinking and blithely ignoring any negatives. It is about looking at things positively, yet realistically. It involves acknowledging any possible setbacks or difficulties and planning how to deal with these in a positive way. Optimistic thinking alone is also associated with underestimating risks (Peterson and Park 2003) and further research has shown that extreme optimism can lead to overconfidence (Ifcher and Zarghamee 2011).

In general, humans tend to have a 'negativity bias' – a tendency to notice the more negative things, people and events. We are all more likely to remember the one negative comment we received, rather than the ten positive ones, or remember the bad day of our holiday rather than the six positive days! This negativity bias has developed as it has been evolutionary adaptive for our species – noticing dangers, fear and anger has been necessary in the past for the survival of the human species.

Hope, optimism and autism

So, although we can all have a tendency to focus on the negatives, there can be some specific challenges for individuals on the autism spectrum and some evidence does suggest that individuals on the autism spectrum may be more susceptible to a negativity bias when it comes to forming beliefs about future outcomes (Kuzmanovic, Rigoux and Vogeley 2016). Some specific challenges for individuals on the autism spectrum in having an optimistic outlook can include:

- **Literal thinking.** A literal interpretation of language and events can lead to possible misunderstandings and corresponding negative expectations about future events.

- **Difficulties with social interaction.** If individuals frequently find it difficult to socialise with others or have a history of previous misunderstandings, they might feel less confident about future situations.

- **Environmental and sensory sensitivities.** These can increase anxiety and general levels of frustration in individuals on the autism spectrum, making it harder to think hopefully.

- **Low self-esteem.** This can affect levels of confidence and belief about the future.

- **Fear of failure.** Some individuals on the autism spectrum may have perfectionist tendencies. In combination with low self-esteem and overgeneralising ('I have failed this test so I'm a failure in all aspects of life') this can lead to restricting beliefs and behaviours about the future.

- **Executive functioning.** Executive functioning involves the skills needed in planning, sequencing, organising, prioritising, remembering and carrying out tasks. This can be an area of difficulty for some individuals on the autism spectrum (Attwood 2007) and can affect how they approach future goals.

- **Need for sameness and routine.** This can mean some individuals on the autism spectrum may not look forward to future events – the anxiety about change can outweigh any excitement they might feel.

- **Theory of mind.** It can be difficult for individuals on the autism spectrum to understand and predict other people's (and their own) thoughts, feelings and perspectives.

Although there are a number of challenges which it is important to bear in mind, many autistic individuals do develop positive and optimistic attitudes. Let's look at how to support young people to do this.

HOPE AND OPTIMISM: PUTTING IT INTO PRACTICE
Group activities

OPTIMIST VERSUS PESSIMIST

(11–14, 14–16, 16–18)

Aim: For students to understand the difference between optimism and pessimism.

Resources: Download and print the 'Optimist vs. Pessimist Cards' from Appendix E.

How to do it: Students can work with a partner, or in groups of twos, making up a small group of four students.

1. Explain what is meant by optimism (feeling good about the future and expecting a positive outcome) and pessimism (feeling negative about the future and expecting a negative outcome).

2. Give each pair of students sticky notes with 'optimist' and 'pessimist' written on. Students decide who will take on each role first, but will have the opportunity to change halfway through the activity.

3. Now give each pair of students the statements below (or adapt them to meet the level and interests of your group). Students take each statement in turn with the 'optimist' suggesting an optimistic approach to the situation and the 'pessimist' suggesting a pessimistic approach. Example:

   Statement: 'We are going on a school trip to the museum tomorrow.'

   Optimist: 'This could be fun. We get to visit the museum and learn lots of new things. There will be interesting displays to look at and activities to do. We will be able to see how people lived in the past. I am looking forward to it. It is something different.'

   Pessimist: 'Oh no, a school trip. It's going to be awful. It will be the most boring day ever. I hate museums and this one will be the worst I have ever visited. I'm going to hate it and be bored all day. I won't learn anything at all.'

4. Halfway through, ask the students to swap roles so that all get an opportunity to practise optimistic and pessimistic responses.

5. Once all statements have been discussed, bring the group back together and ask for some demonstrations of examples. Discuss what the benefits of optimistic thinking are. What can too much pessimistic thinking lead to?

FROM UNHOPEFUL TO HOPEFUL

(11–14, 14–16, 16–18)

Aim: To illustrate how unhopeful thinking patterns can be changed to more hopeful thoughts.

Resources: Download and print the 'Unhopeful Statements' from Appendix F and cut into small cards.

How to do it:

1. Explain to students that how we talk to ourselves, influences our thoughts and behaviours. If we speak in hopeful language to ourselves we have more chance of behaving in a hopeful manner and working towards our goals. If our self-talk is unhopeful, then we have less chance of doing this. Hopeful talk focuses on the opportunities that are available.

2. Divide students up so they are working with a supportive partner. Give each pair the 'unhopeful' statements from below. Ask students to work together to create a more hopeful version of the same problem. Give an example to demonstrate this.

3. Once students have finished, feed back examples to the bigger group. Reiterate the effectiveness of hopeful talk and how this can lead to us being better able to focus on moving towards goals. Ask students if they can think of any examples that they hear themselves thinking or saying regularly (e.g. 'I'm not good at maths', 'I'm not good with talking to people'). What would be more hopeful versions? Challenge students to notice when they are thinking or saying these unhopeful statements over the next week – can they catch themselves (or each other!) and use more positive language?

UNHOPEFUL STATEMENTS (FOLLOWED BY EXAMPLES OF HOPEFUL STATEMENTS)

- I can't do maths. (I am finding this maths topic difficult but I can ask for help and improve.)

- I don't understand what to do in science. (Science is difficult for me to understand but I can ask the teacher for help and listen carefully to what she says.)

- Break times are boring. (I find being on the playground boring but I could go to art club which I find more interesting.)

- I'm too nervous to present my work in class. (I have done good work in class but speaking in front of people is scary. I can ask my teacher if I could present it jointly with a friend.)

- I made a mess of giving a presentation today. (I didn't do as well as I would have liked giving a presentation today but I have learned to make notes before the next time and will get better every time I practise.)

- My friends hate me. (I have had a disagreement with my friends today but we can discuss it and make up.)

- My homework is too hard. (I think my homework is going to be difficult tonight but I will have a good look at the instructions and ask my family to explain it to me if I still don't understand.)

- I'm no good at swimming. (I'm not very confident at swimming yet, but I can get better at it if I practise.)

- The teacher doesn't like me. (The teacher forgot to answer my question today but I can ask it again next lesson.)

THE BEST AND THE WORST CASE SCENARIO

(11–14, 14–16, 16–18)

Aim: To demonstrate the benefits of realistic, yet optimistic thinking in preparing for events.

Resources: Scenarios below printed onto cards or displayed on a projector.

How to do it: This activity asks students to consider the 'best case scenario' and the 'worst case scenario' of a situation. They then use this to help them to identify possible difficulties along the way and how these obstacles can be overcome.

1. Do an example as a class, before giving the scenarios to small groups or pairs of students to discuss. Explain that for each situation students have to consider what the absolutely best outcome could be, and then the absolute worst. Example: Giving a presentation in front of a large audience.

    • Best case: You speak confidently and loudly, your presentation is clear and informative, the audience are very interested and engaged, you make the audience laugh, people applaud at the end, everybody asks relevant questions, you feel relaxed, people give you good feedback.

    • Worst case: You go bright red and forget everything you were going to say. You speak in a whisper and nobody can hear you. The audience looks bored and begin yawning and fidgeting. Nobody asks any questions and nobody claps. You trip over your own feet on stage and your trousers fall down.

2. Once students have had chance to discuss the best and the worst possibilities (encourage them to be as creative as they like!), explain that these extremes do not usually happen, usually the event will fit somewhere between the two. Explain how considering the worst can help us to prepare and overcome any potential difficulties. Now ask each pair of students to take one scenario and to use the 'worst case' to identify three positive things that they could do to help them overcome these difficulties. Example:

- Giving a presentation. Three things to do: Make notes or cue cards so you do not forget what to say. Practise your presentation so that you feel more confident. Wear comfortable clothing that you feel confident in.

SCENARIOS

- Giving a presentation.
- Attending an after-school club.
- Going to your first swimming lesson.
- Having a big project to do for homework.
- Moving to a new school.
- Going to a friend's birthday party.
- Taking part in a charity fun run.
- Going to the dentist for a check-up.
- Walking to school for the first time on your own.
- Going for an interview for a part-time job.

Individual activities

FUTURE HOPES

(7–11, 11–14, 14–16, 16–18)

Aim: To increase feelings of hope and optimism about the future.

Resources: Art and craft materials; photographs; old magazines; internet.

How to do it: This activity aims to support students to focus on future hopes and goals in order to increase feelings of hope and optimism. It acts as a basis for further activities in this chapter and in Chapter 6 on resilience and growth mindset. Before students can begin to put into place the goal-setting and motivation techniques outlined later in this book, they first need to have identified hopes that are important to them. Having hopes and dreams for the future can also help to increase feelings of wellbeing.

1. Ask students to make a 'vision board' with the title 'What is important to me now'. This can be done using craft materials, or using a computer. Encourage them to be as creative as they like in how they present these. They might like to think about the following categories: pets, family, friends, other important people, school, hobbies, interests, favourite things, community or voluntary activities.

2. Now ask students to make a similar vision board with the title 'What is important to me in the future'. Encourage them to think short term (e.g. the following term or next school year) and longer term (when they reach adulthood). Some students may benefit from being shown a visual timeline of the future, showing the ages that they are likely to leave school or college or begin work. Encourage students to consider all aspects of their lives: education, learning, work, hobbies, interests, holiday, living circumstances, home, pets, friends, family, learning to drive...

3. Do not worry too much if students do not have many long-term goals – they might not be ready to think that far ahead. Some autistic individuals also have difficulty with predicting feelings and emotions which can make forward planning difficult. Others may not want to share their hopes, or some just may not yet have the knowledge or experience of jobs, careers and independent living to be able to consider this aspect of their lives. This in itself can highlight possible next steps for the student (e.g. additional input on careers advice).

4. The vision boards can be used for later activities to help the student to identify their personal goals. Remind students that vision boards are 'working documents'. As they grow

older and gain new experiences, they might like to add new hopes and dreams, or remove some of their old ones.

CHALLENGING UNHOPEFUL SELF-TALK

(7–11, 11–14, 14–16, 16–18)

Aim: To challenge unhopeful thoughts and opinions which act as a barrier to the individual from making progress and from feeling optimistic.

Resources: Pens and paper. Computer software (optional).

How to do it: This activity helps the student to generate more optimistic self-talk about an event, situation or thought.

1. Ask the student to identify an event, situation or thought which the student is 'unhopeful' or pessimistic about (e.g. 'I'm rubbish at maths', 'There's no point me doing this test as I'll fail', 'I don't want to go to tennis camp as I won't get on with the others', 'I'm always left out at parties').

2. Begin by focusing on the positives. Ask the student what is going well in their life. Ask them what they have been enjoying and what they think they are getting better at. Which skills and strengths do they feel they possess? Some students may benefit from creating a spider diagram or list at this point to give them a visual reminder of what is going well and the resources they have to draw on.

3. Next ask them to identify the problem and to be as specific as possible. Rather than 'I'm rubbish at maths', ask questions to pull out the specifics (e.g. 'I'm good at some topics in maths but I have not been understanding fractions and decimals. I can do the work in the lesson but can't do my homework and did badly in the last test'). This makes the problem more specific and manageable.

4. Now 'challenge' some of the unhopeful thoughts that the student has generated. It is important to do this in a neutral way so that it is not interpreted as being critical or unhelpful! Try asking questions such as:

- What evidence do you have for that?

- What evidence do you have against that thought?

- When has this not been the case?

- When have you felt more optimistic about this?

- When has this gone well in the past?

- What advice would you give a friend who was saying this?

- How would your superhero (if the student created a superhero in Chapter 4) think about this situation?

5. Now support the student to reframe their unhopeful talk into more hopeful talk (e.g. 'I'm rubbish at maths' becomes 'I didn't do as well as usual in the last maths test but I can attend after-school homework club to help me understand fractions and do better next time as this has helped me in the past'). If students identify practical things that they could do, support them to put these steps into place.

6. Remind the student of their more hopeful thoughts if you hear them returning to their less helpful thoughts.

OPTIMISTIC PLANNING

(11–14, 14–16, 16–18)

Aim: To understand how to plan optimistically and realistically.

Resources: Planning sheet (Appendix G).

How to do it: Choose an upcoming event or situation which the student is not feeling hopeful or optimistic about, perhaps an exam or test, a school trip, or a social event with friends.

1. Discuss the upcoming event with the student. Ask them for specifics about the event or situation and how they feel about it. Give the student a copy of Appendix G, the planning sheet.

2. Now talk through the planning sheet with the student, working on one box at a time. Encourage the student to generate their own ideas; the role of the adult is to prompt and clarify, rather than producing all of the ideas.

3. Ensure that the next steps identified are specific and clear. Be explicit about what the student needs to do next and about any mini-deadlines.

4. After the event, review the planning sheet. How did the event go in the end? Was it as scary or as unpleasant as the student had initially anticipated? What were the positives in the situation? Did any of the obstacles surface and, if so, did the student put the suggested strategies into place? How did these work? Will they use them again or adapt them in future?

Depending on the age and ability of the student, this activity can be used in different ways. Some students may start small, with smaller events that they are worried about (e.g. going to buy a snack from the school canteen), while others may use 'bigger' events which require more planning and to be broken down into smaller steps. Older students may like to use this planning sheet independently, or to keep an electronic version on their mobile device to refer to. Some students may like to use pictures rather than words.

Adult communication

Model hopeful self-talk

Let children and young people see the adults around them also using hopeful self-talk! Change your 'I can't play chess' to 'I haven't learned how to play chess yet.'

Model 'I wonder...' rather than 'I hope...'

This is a simple trick which can help to make uncertainty more comfortable (Burkeman 2017). Saying 'I hope…' (e.g. 'I hope I get on the school football team') defines only one outcome as acceptable. Using 'I wonder…' (e.g. 'I wonder if I will get on the school football team this year' or 'I wonder which extracurricular activities I will enjoy this year') is more open-ended and keeps you more receptive to new possibilities. Model this way of talking in your own speech and support this way of thinking in your students too.

Responding to 'the eternal pessimist'

You may come across students, whether or not on the autism spectrum, who are the eternal pessimist, despite your best efforts. Remember that it can take time to change fixed ways of thinking, so do not give up too soon! Model more optimistic ways of thinking in your responses, so that the student and other students, are exposed to this more helpful way of thinking. Be aware also that one very pessimistic student may have a negative impact on the rest of the group and can influence others' perceptions of the situation. In this case it can be especially important to do some specific work on optimistic thinking with the whole group.

Remember too that adults, again whether or not on the autism spectrum, can also be pessimistic. Have you ever worked with a colleague who only ever sees the negatives? It can be worth considering which staff work with children and young people as pessimism can be contagious!

Responding to 'ever the optimist'

At the other end of the scale, you may encounter students who are far too optimistic! Although this may sound like a good thing, these students may have exaggerated hopes about how events will unfold and may not feel it necessary to prepare for situations – leading to disappointment and frustration. It can be just as important to complete activities on optimism with these students, focusing on realistic optimism and ensuring that they focus on effective planning and goal-setting techniques.

Support executive functioning

Children and teens on the autism spectrum can have difficulty with 'executive functioning' (Attwood 2007). This involves seeing the 'bigger picture' and being able to plan, prioritise, organise, sequence, remember and carry out the stages within a task. There are many easy strategies you can use to support students to develop these skills. Show them how to make 'to-do' lists and cross off each task once complete. Teach students how to set reminders or alarms on their mobile phones to remind them to complete tasks. Show students how to use diaries, planners and calendars to prepare for upcoming events. Within the classroom or home setting try using 'task boards' to break down a larger activity into smaller steps, using pictures or words depending on the student.

FLOW AND OTHER POSITIVE STATES

'Flow' is a term coined by positive psychologist Mikhail Csikszentmihalyi and is considered to be another key element of human flourishing.

YOUR TURN

Have you ever felt so absorbed in what you were doing that you lost track of what you were doing and did not notice what was happening around you? Make a list of the times that you have experienced this. Which activities were you engaged in?

If you could answer the previous question you have probably experienced what positive psychologists call 'flow', the experience of being totally absorbed in what you were doing. Individuals experience 'flow' through different activities – perhaps though work-related tasks, playing chess, dancing, playing tennis, household chores, painting, rock-climbing – or through many other tasks. Being immersed in 'flow' has been likened to being effortlessly pulled forward like the flow of a river, hence the name. Athletes often refer to 'being in the zone' – when they talk about this they are referring to being in 'flow'. You do not have to be a world-class athlete to experience it; we can all experience flow whatever our age, background, or activity we are engaged in. Perhaps you have been so absorbed in a book that you look up at the clock and realise several hours have passed since you opened it, or been so involved in a task at work that you realised three hours had passed and you had been totally oblivious to what was going on around you, or even to physical sensations such as hunger or fatigue. Your mind did not wander, but you were so focused and concentrated on the task that you lost awareness of everything else. These are both examples of flow.

Flow experiences share some important characteristics (Csikszentmihalyi 1992):

- Complete concentration on the task in hand at the present moment – the mind is not wandering or thinking about the past or future.

- Clear goals and immediate feedback. You know what it is you need to focus on and are getting immediate feedback on your progress (e.g. in a sport you know if you are winning or losing).

- Feeling 'at one' with the activity. Your actions and awareness become merged so that you do not feel separate from the task. A musician, for example, may become the music that he plays, with the involvement feeling almost effortless.

- Loss of self-consciousness. You may lose awareness of yourself and experience feelings of calm and serenity.

- A sense of control over what you are doing; you feel that you know what to do next and do not worry about failure.

- Time passing in different ways. Time seems to 'fly by' without you realising.

- Intrinsic motivation. You feel that what you are doing is rewarding for its own sake, with other end goals being less important.

The sense of flow also happens under specific circumstances – the activity needs to be well matched to our level of skill. If the challenge is too difficult for our skill level, then we are less likely to experience flow as we will find the task too hard and can feel anxious about this. If the challenge is too easy for our skill level then there is a good chance we will become bored. So flow usually occurs when we are engaged in something that challenges us, but at a level which it is just possible for us to meet. Therefore watching TV is not usually considered to be an activity which generates flow due to its passivity. However, blind people often quote television watching as a flow activity (Boniwell 2008) as it is more challenging for them – they have to build mental images of what is going on in the absence of being able to see the screen.

Flow is also considered beneficial because of its lasting effects – when we are in 'flow' we do not notice it, but afterwards we will feel happier, fulfilled and have a sense of achievement.

Is flow always a good thing?

The benefits of flow are that it is enjoyable, is associated with optimal performance and enhances motivation as flow activities are intrinsically motivating. However, there are also some potential pitfalls.

- Some 'flow' activities may be morally concerning (e.g. gambling).

- Some 'flow' activities can become addictive (e.g. computer games) – this can have a negative impact on the individual's life, and can make life without the addiction feel boring and meaningless.

So it is not only important to learn how to make flow happen in order to enhance wellbeing, but also to learn how to manage it so that we can let go when necessary.

Flow and the autism spectrum

Many children and young people on the autism spectrum have a 'special interest', an interest which they are passionate and intense about. The 'special interest' often plays a large part in their lives, it may dominate their time, thoughts and conversation. A 'special' interest goes much further than a regular hobby or interest. Some special interests may appear unusual to the observer – there can often be an emphasis on collecting, cataloguing and categorising. There may be repetitive actions and behaviours, set routines around the special interest or a huge factual knowledge of related statistics. Special interests can range from quantum physics to collecting bottle tops. Whatever the interest, it can be an opportunity for individuals to reduce stress, increase feelings of wellbeing and experience flow. Research suggests that some of the repetitive activities which accompany special interests can help to achieve a 'flow' state of mind (McDonell and Milton 2014).

However, as mentioned above, some hobbies and interests can be more addictive (e.g. computer games) – these are actually designed to optimise flow and keep people playing. This can then have a negative impact on other areas of life – homework may not get done, players may get insufficient sleep, may spend less time being with people, may neglect other important tasks (such as washing) – which can then lead to a lower mood and frustration. Some evidence suggests that children on the autism spectrum or with related difficulties such as attention deficit hyperactivity disorder (ADHD) can be more susceptible to screen addiction (Kutscher 2016).

There can also be some additional difficulties for young people on the autism spectrum. A rigidity of thought and less social awareness may mean they are less inclined to try new things or may not see the importance of stopping work on their special interest for other tasks (such as to shower, study or be with friends).

Other positive states

Different to 'flow', another positive state is that of savouring. Martin Seligman (2002), one of the leaders of the positive psychology movement, says that the ability to savour positive experiences is one of the most important aspects of happiness. Savouring is engaging in thoughts and behaviours which allow us to generate, intensify and prolong enjoyment of a situation. This leads to positive emotions and increases our overall wellbeing. Whereas flow is a state in which the individual is almost unaware of their surroundings and emotions, savouring is the opposite – the individual is acutely aware of their surroundings and the positive emotions these are creating.

KEY TERM

Savouring. Deliberately attending to and appreciating positive experiences. Using all of the senses to become immersed and really enjoy what is going on.

Twenty-first-century life is not always conducive to savouring experiences! It can often be the norm to rush through activities and multitask, with the aim of saving time. How often have you walked while talking on your mobile phone, later to realise you hadn't noticed any of your surroundings? Or eaten dinner when watching television or working at a screen, only to realise your food has gone before you noticed? Walk down any busy high street and you will observe many examples of people not 'savouring' – those with music piping through earphones to block out their surroundings, those talking on hands-free equipment while completing another task, or individuals so concerned with taking selfies or photos that they are not savouring the moment at the time. Internal distractions can also prevent us savouring situations – perhaps our brains are taken up with worry, anxiety or other ruminating thoughts which mean we are not truly 'present'.

So, sometimes it can be useful to make 'savouring' a deliberate act; by paying more attention to one thing at a time, we can find that there are many pleasurable experiences to notice in our everyday lives – which can increase feelings of wellbeing and satisfaction.

Autism and single-tasking

In the busy twenty-first century we are often encouraged to multitask. It is rare that we focus on just one thing at a time. Even when driving we may be listening to an audiobook or talking hands free. When working on a computer we may have multiple webpages, emails and instant messaging sites open. In an open plan office we may be working, talking to colleagues, listening to the radio and eating our lunch, all at the same time. Researchers are now realising that all of this multitasking may not be positive for our wellbeing and there are numerous books and resources available about mindfulness, concentrating on the present moment and on one thing at a time.

Individuals on the autism spectrum can often have difficulties switching attention from one thing to another (Attwood 2007); it can be much harder for them to 'change track' from one activity to another, whereas peers may be appear able to shift attention with ease from one thing to the next and back again. This is sometimes considered to be a problem, particularly in the classroom where attention needs to shift quickly from one task to the next. It is important to be aware of this and realise that the child or young person in question is not deliberately ignoring instructions, but has considerable difficulties shifting attention to a new task if the first has not yet been completed (Attwood 2007).

When considering 'flow' or 'savouring' activities, or indeed many everyday situations, with children and young people on the autism spectrum, it is important to take into account their differences in shifting attention and multitasking.

FLOW AND OTHER POSITIVE STATES: PUTTING IT INTO PRACTICE

Some of the following activities focus on 'flow' – both helping children and young people on the autism spectrum to build in more regular experiences of flow to develop a greater sense of wellbeing, and supporting them to manage 'flow' activities. It is easier to achieve flow in activities which we self-select and which are intrinsically motivating, so therefore it can be challenging to try to force flow in formal learning settings. Other activities investigate savouring and noticing the world around us.

Group activities

IDENTIFY 'FLOW'

(7–11, 11–14, 14–16, 16–18)

Aim: To support students to identify activities that generate 'flow' for them.

Resources: Sticky notes.

How to do it:

1. Begin by explaining to students what is meant by 'flow' – this is when we are engaged in a fulfilling and engaging activity which absorbs us. It often happens when we are doing fulfilling work, engaged in a creative hobby, play a sport or playing a musical instrument. It is likely to be different for each one of us. Many sportspeople call it 'being in the zone'. It is a pleasant state, when we feel

no anxiety. It usually comes about when we are doing something which is challenging for us, but not too difficult.

2. Ask students to consider any times when they feel they have experienced this, it may be things they do regularly, or at times when they were younger. Ask them to write or draw each one on a sticky note. Next ask students to discuss their ideas with a partner. They can tell their partner why they enjoyed the activities they have identified.

3. Students then add their sticky notes to a group poster. Discuss the sticky notes which have been presented, emphasising that we all have different activities which give us 'flow'.

4. Finally, ask students to discuss with their partner if there are any activities they would like to do more of, or any that they would like to try out, now that they have heard the suggestions of others. Ask for feedback – this list may provide ideas for future after-school clubs, day trips or other activities.

TRYING OUT SOMETHING NEW

(7–11, 11–14, 14–16, 16–18)

Aim: To encourage students to try out new activities, and for students to have the opportunity to share their interests with others.

Resources: (Depending on the group) Projector, presentation software, large poster paper, videos, other resources.

How to do it:

1. Explain to students that we all have different activities and interests which we enjoy doing. This activity is an

opportunity to share interests with others in the group and give them a chance to try out things which we enjoy.

2. Ask students to identify an interest or hobby which they enjoy doing. The first thing they are to do is to plan how they would like to share this with the rest of the group. Depending on the interest or hobby, they might like to give a demonstration, show work they have produced, show a video or give a presentation about their interest. Allow students sufficient time to gather any necessary resources or create a poster or presentation to share with the group.

3. In the next session students share their interest or hobby with the group. Although some may be willing to talk in front of the group, other ways of presenting should also be allowed – such as showing a presentation or poster, or sharing their hobby from around a table rather than having to stand in front of an 'audience'.

4. The overall aim of this activity is not just to give students the opportunity to share their interests, but also to try out new activities. So, for example, if a student has shared their cross-stitching hobby, students should then have the opportunity to try this out. The resources and logistics needed for this will need to be prepared in advance.

STOP AND SAVOUR

(7–11, 11–14, 14–16, 16–18)

Aim: To explore how we often go through the day on 'auto-pilot' without noticing many of the things around us.

Resources: Music (classical music often works well), raisins or other dried fruit, a garden or park, the classroom (all optional, other spaces and objects can work just as well).

How to do it: This task is made up of a number of short activities which can be done during one lesson, or spread out across the week. The aim is to help students to appreciate small experiences and pleasures which they might not usually notice. Autistic students who experience sensory discomfort may find it difficult to focus on background music, for example, if there are lots of other sounds in the environment – this can all become overwhelming. These activities are ways of enabling students to focus on just one thing at a time. Older students may like to discuss in more detail why we often go through life on autopilot and why we attempt to multitask. Choose from some of the following activities:

- Play a piece of music and ask students to close their eyes and just listen for a few moments without doing anything else. Which instruments could they hear? Play the piece again and ask them if they can identify any other instruments the second time around. How did they feel about the music? Did it remind them of anything? Point out that there is often background music playing which we do not really listen to.

- Give students a raisin (or other fruit, or popcorn also often works well – something with an interesting texture). Be aware that some students on the autism spectrum may have sensory preferences which mean that certain textures, smells or tastes are uncomfortable for them. Ask students to look carefully at the food in their hands for a few moments, noticing any details, then smell the food, feel it and slowly place it in their mouths, biting it slowly and noticing the flavour, before swallowing. Spend a few moments on each of these steps. Did the students notice anything new about the food that they have never noticed before?

- Ask students to look around the classroom in silence for a few minutes, asking them to notice three things that they have not noticed before. After the few minutes are up, ask students to feed back. What did they notice? (*A crack on the ceiling, a poster they have never looked at, a sign they have never noticed, a change in paint colour...*) Why do we often not notice things in our everyday environment? (Some students on the autism spectrum can be very good at observing detail and noticing when small things are out of place!)

- If possible, take students outside to a garden or park. Ask them to sit with their eyes closed for a few moments in silence and just listen. Which sounds can they identify? Ask students to feed back. Were they surprised at the things that they could hear? We often don't notice all of the sounds in our environment if we are busy thinking about something. (Some students on the autism spectrum may hear everything and find it difficult to distinguish the different sounds – they might find this activity challenging but it can be useful to help them to recognise any particular difficulties.)

- Ask students to look carefully at a flower, leaf, bird, tree or other natural object for a few moments. Ask them to focus on the detail. What did they notice? It can be surprising to look at a flower, for example, in detail – were students surprised at how many petals there were or at how these are arranged?

GET CRAFTY

(7–11, 11–14, 14–16, 16–18)

Aim: To explore crafting as a means of promoting flow and feelings of wellbeing.

Resources: Various craft materials.

How to do it: Studies have shown that crafting can boost wellbeing and that engaging with arts and crafts can lead to increased calm, energy and happiness the next day (Connor, DeYoung and Silvia 2016). Many young people in the twenty-first century spend the majority of their free time onscreen, rather than engaging in more traditional pastimes. Support them to experience a greater range of arts and crafts activities and help them to identify whether there are any they would like to pursue further.

- Arts and crafts make a great activity for break and lunchtimes, particularly when the weather is poor. Card-making, knitting, crochet, pottery, origami, jewellery making, model painting – all of these things can be adapted for different age groups and interests.

- After-school clubs are also ideal for creating these sorts of opportunities – perhaps ask a specialist to lead the group, or ask around your staff team. You might find that there are many hidden talents and individuals willing to share their skills.

- Art and crafts activities can also be a great way for students on the autism spectrum to socialise with others, in a less threatening environment. Many autistic individuals have difficulty with unstructured socialising, but more 'structured' socialising, over a joint activity, can be easier; there is less pressure to talk and the emphasis is on the activity rather than socialising.

- Provide support. Some students may feel confident to try out their own thing, while others will want to copy from an example. Provide clear visual instructions or a demonstration to help students to get started. Provide support but at the same time promote independence –

encourage students to have a go. Arts and crafts are not about making something perfect, but about experimenting and getting better through trial and error.

Individual activities

USING AND MANAGING SPECIAL INTERESTS

(7–11, 11–14, 14–16, 16–18)

Aim: To support individual students to identify 'flow' activities or 'special interests' and how they can use these positively in their lives.

Resources: Various, depending on the individual student.

How to do it: Some students on the autism spectrum may have 'special interests'. These can be interests or hobbies which the student is extremely passionate and knowledgeable about. The interest or activity may dominate the student's life, making it difficult to focus on other tasks. Interests may be 'typical' interests (*Star Wars*, a soap opera, animals, football league tables...) taken to an extreme level, or may stand out as being more unusual (collecting bottle tops, a cartoon character which is not age appropriate...). Hyperfocus on a special interest can, at best, lead to individuals becoming an expert in their field. It may lead to a fulfilling career or hobby in which they excel. The negative side can be that exclusive focus on an interest may lead to other aspects of life being neglected (e.g. doing homework, household chores, eating properly, neglecting friendships). This activity encourages students to reflect on the possible positive and negative aspects of their interest, and to consider if it is beginning to dominate their life and have a negative effect.

1. Draw or write the student's interest in the middle of a large sheet of paper. To one side of the paper ask the student to list all of the positive aspects of their interest. Support

them to generate ideas (e.g. positive feelings, increased happiness, interest in the subject, opportunity to learn new skills, achievements).

2. On the other side of the paper, ask the student to list if there are any possible negatives to their hobby or interest (e.g. not getting homework done and getting into trouble, forgetting to eat dinner, negative reactions from others). There may be no negatives and that is fine – leave the activity here!

3. Explain to the student how having interests is a good thing and there are many benefits; you are not trying to get them to stop spending time on their interest, but helping them to manage it so that they do not neglect other important aspects of life and do not become frustrated by the demands of others which may interfere with their interest. Some students may argue that they do not feel these other aspects of their life are important. Explain calmly, using a visual flow chart if helpful, what the long-term impact may be. So, for example, if a student says he would rather watch his favourite television show on the internet instead of doing homework, but wants to go to university to study media, then show how not doing homework can lead to getting poorer results at school and therefore not achieving the grades needed to enter university.

4. Identify one specific aspect that the student would like to work on (e.g. getting homework done so that they avoid getting into trouble for this). Work with the student to identify three possible solutions. Example:

- Go to lunchtime homework club and do it then.

- Do my homework as soon as I get home from school instead of turning on the internet.

- Set an alarm for 6pm each evening to remind me to start my homework.

5. Next identify the pros and cons of each solution.

- Go to homework club at lunchtime

- Pros: I won't have any homework to do at home.

- Cons: I don't really feel like doing more homework at lunchtime.

6. Once pros and cons for each solution have been identified, ask the student to choose which one they would like to try. Help them to make this as specific as possible (e.g. when, how, how often, what support they need). Create a small action plan, stating exactly what the student will do and what you will do to help them.

7. Review progress a week later. What has gone well? Has the problem been reduced? Does the student need to try one of the other possible solutions instead?

8. Remember that special interests can help students on the autism spectrum to experience feelings of happiness, relaxation and fulfilment. The aim of this activity is not to reduce the time spent on interests, but to ensure that students are able to manage other necessary aspects of life such as getting sufficient sleep, taking care of personal hygiene and meeting other important commitments.

MOVE OVER, ANXIETY!

(7–11, 11–14, 14–16, 16–18)

Aim: To help students to identify anxieties, worries or other feelings which stop them from enjoying experiences and opportunities which they would like to.

Resources: Download and print Appendix H (if needed).

How to do it: Some students on the autism spectrum may find that there are experiences that they would like to try out or enjoy (e.g. going to gymnastics club, spending time with friends, walking the dog) but they do not because they feel so overwhelmed by feelings of embarrassment, worry or anxiety. These can stop them from being 'in the present' and enjoying the moment. These feelings and reasons are going to vary from individual to individual and each student will likely need solutions unique to them. This activity merely acts as a starting point to facilitate discussion and empower the student to begin to identify coping strategies.

1. Identify the situation which the student would like to enjoy, but does not (e.g. they would like to help a friend celebrate their birthday but do not enjoy tenpin bowling which is the activity). You can use Appendix H to structure the discussion if needed. Use words or small drawings, depending on what works best for the individual student.

2. Begin with the positives (e.g. the student has been invited to a birthday celebration, appreciates this and values their friend, they would like to help their friend celebrate and would like to join in).

3. Help the student to identify what they do enjoy about the situation or what goes well (e.g. 'I enjoy making a birthday card and wrapping a present for my friend, am able to get the bus independently to the bowling alley, I know what to expect when there, they are a nice group of people who help me to feel included').

4. Next help the student to identify why they do not end up enjoying the situation (e.g. 'I find the place too noisy, I can't hear what people are saying and I don't join in the conversation, I find the party goes on too long and I am ready to leave after 20 minutes, by the time we go for ice cream afterwards I have run out of things to say').

5. Support the student to identify their own solutions or coping strategies (e.g. telling the friend that they find the bowling alley uncomfortable but will join them for ice cream afterwards, just attending for a short time). Coping strategies may include strategies to cope with sensory discomfort (e.g. ear plugs, tinted lenses, change of location) or assertiveness techniques to inform others of their preferences and needs.

Adult communication

Encourage 'savouring'

There are many moments to savour during everyday life. Try drawing attention to some of these as and when they occur. Perhaps you catch an unusual birdsong, see an interesting flower, hear an intriguing piece of music on the radio, spot some street art, or come across an interesting design – whatever it is, encourage the students you are working with to notice it too and to focus on it for a few moments with no other objective but to enjoy the moment.

Build in opportunities to single task

We live in a multitasking world in which many people, wrongly, believe that multitasking will speed things up. These habits can be hard to break so encourage your students to single task whenever possible. This will support them to be more able to enjoy each separate activity. Have a 'no technology at snack/meal times' policy and show students how to complete one task at a time rather than trying to do two at once.

Enable 'flow' experiences

Some researchers (Fox Eades 2008) suggest that children in school do not achieve 'flow' as much as we would like. There may be a number of reasons for this, including the frequent interruptions, pressure to complete tasks within set time frames and quick transitions from activity to activity. Be aware of barriers in your setting which may be preventing children and young people from experiencing flow. This may include making a conscious effort not to interrupt flow-friendly activities.

GRATITUDE AND APPRECIATION

Studies have shown that being grateful is associated with happiness, wellbeing and life satisfaction (Emmons 2007; Lyubomirsky 2007). Gratitude is about not taking life for granted and works on different levels – being grateful to people, being grateful to life for something or as a tendency to experience gratitude across situations.

Gratitude interventions (such as counting blessings, being thankful and recording what went well) have been investigated with powerful results. Such interventions have been shown to increase happiness and reduce depressive symptoms for up to six months (Seligman *et al.* 2005). Studies with children using a school-based gratitude diary have been shown to increase feelings of belonging towards school (Diebel 2014).

Recognising feelings of gratitude can help us to focus on the good things in our lives and therefore helps to increase our wellbeing and level of life satisfaction.

Kindness and gratitude

Kindness is about doing nice things for other people, not for our own personal benefit, but for the positive impact on the other person. Research shows that doing kind acts for others makes people happier. There can be a number of reasons for this – doing kind acts for others can help us to connect with them, and can also help us to feel more confident and optimistic about our ability to make a difference. Kind acts also help us to feel more positive about other people and the community we live in (Lyubomirsky, Sheldon and Schkade 2005). So kindness has been shown to have a benefit for both the 'giver' and the 'receiver'.

However, when talking about kindness, it is important to remember that the focus should be on the benefit to the other person, and not just to the person 'doing' the kind act. There are many books, projects and websites now dedicated to 'random acts of kindness' and, while these generally advocate doing kind deeds for others, the focus should always be on the impact on the other person, and not about doing kind acts for more self-centred reasons of increasing our own happiness levels!

Gratitude and autism

When working with students on the autism spectrum, it is important not to try and impose 'neurotypical' beliefs and opinions. Some of the things that a neurotypical child or young person may feel grateful for (e.g. being able to spend the day chatting to their friends) may not be important for a student on the autism spectrum (e.g. who may be grateful for the opposite – having the opportunity to spend a day by themselves!). There are no right or wrong answers when it comes to gratitude and it is important you do not try to 'force' a young person on the autism spectrum to be grateful for something which does not have meaning for them as this can add additional confusion ('I've been told I *should* be grateful to play with my friends, but really I just want to read my book. What's wrong with me?').

Many students on the autism spectrum have difficulty in interpreting other people's thoughts and intentions (difficulties with 'theory of mind'), and, equally, many neurotypical people can also have difficulty in interpreting the thoughts and perspectives of autistic people! This can sometimes lead to difficulties with gratitude from both sides. For example, an intended act of kindness may be interpreted as having the opposite effect. Example:

- Suzy, a student on the autism spectrum, sees that a friend is upset. She leaves her alone, as this is what she would like others to do with her – when she is upset the last thing that she feels like doing is having to cope with communicating with other people. However, her friend thinks that Suzy was not being supportive and did not care about her being upset.

GRATITUDE AND APPRECIATION: PUTTING IT INTO PRACTICE
Group activities

CLASS GRATITUDE TREE

(7–11, 11–14, 14–16)

Aim: To encourage students to identify and recognise things that they are grateful for.

Resources: Display board, coloured paper cut into 'leaves', craft materials.

How to do it:

1. Create a 'gratitude tree'. This could be a picture of a tree on a display board, or even a 3D tree made out of a large branch or wire. In this case, leaves can be hung around the branches rather than stuck on to the wall.

2. Explain to students that we all have thing that we are grateful for. These may be people (having a good friend, supportive family member, a good teacher, or a helpful classmate, for example), specific things other people do for us (a classmate lending us a book, somebody holding a door open when we had lots of bags), animals (a dog who is happy to see us), things that we have noticed or appreciated (a sunny day, a beautiful flower, the stars in the sky), things that have happened to us (having an opportunity to go on holiday, winning a prize, being asked to help with something), or more general concepts (having good health, clean water, enough food, a comfortable house). Explain that we can be grateful for big things and small things.

3. Encourage students to think of one thing they are grateful for and to write, or draw, it on a 'leaf' before sticking it on the gratitude tree. Some students might like to share their idea with the rest of the group, or the adult may read out some of the ideas that have been shared.

4. Decide how you are going to add to the 'gratitude tree'. You may decide to have a set time each week that students can add to the tree, or allow students to add leaves as and when feelings of gratitude occur to them. You may like to display the tree in a prominent place and encourage staff and parents to add to the tree too!

5. Try to refer to the tree regularly to encourage regular feelings of gratitude and to highlight any specific acts of kindness and nice things that have been noticed.

THREE GOOD THINGS

(7–11, 11–14, 14–16)

Aim: To support students to recognise good things that have happened, and their role in these good things.

How to do it: This activity may work well if done at a set time each day, or each week (e.g. before home-time, or during tutor-time).

1. Place students into pairs, ensuring that students on the autism spectrum are working with supportive peers.

2. Ask students to each identify three good things that have happened since the previous day/week. These can be big or small, significant or insignificant events. Explain to students that if their partner is struggling to think of three things, they should ask questions and make suggestions to support them with this task.

3. Next ask students to reflect on their role in the 'good things' that have happened. This can help to increase feelings of self-esteem as well as to help students feel that they have an element of agency over their lives. Again, ask students to help their partner to identify their role in the good thing. Examples:

> 'I really enjoyed taking my dog for a walk and watching him chase after the ball. I chose to take him to help my mum out as she was busy.'

> 'I got a better score on my science test than the one last term. This is because I have been spending more time on my science homework.'

> 'I had a great time at after-school trampoline club. I had the confidence to go along and try it out.'

4. It may be appropriate for some students to share some of their thoughts with the larger group, but others may prefer to share just with their partner.

HELPING OTHERS

(11–14, 14–16, 16–18)

Aim: For students to identify how they do/could make a positive difference to the lives of others.

Resources: Large paper, coloured pens.

How to do it:

1. Explain to students that there are many ways in which we can have a positive impact on the lives of others. These can be small everyday acts which are helpful (e.g. helping a friend with their homework, helping a neighbour with their garden), one-off projects (e.g. sending a 'Christmas

shoebox' to a child in another country, taking part in a community tidy-up) or longer-term voluntary or employment activities (e.g. helping out with younger children at a cub scouts group, being a St John Ambulance volunteer, being a firefighter). Making a positive difference to others doesn't always have to involve working directly with people. Looking after rescue animals, training up guide dogs and cleaning up the environment all have a very positive impact on the lives of others.

2. Students work with a supportive partner and write on sticky notes all the things that they have done which have made a difference to others – remember that these can be big or small things! Ask students to write each one on a sticky note and add it to the group poster or display. You may like to display the following list of prompts:

- How have you helped friends?

- How have you helped family and relatives?

- How have you helped neighbours or other people in the community?

- Have you ever helped with fundraising?

- Have you ever done any voluntary work?

- Have you ever donated money/unwanted goods/time to charity?

- Have you done anything to help the environment?

- Have you done any part-time employment or work experience which has helped others?

- Have you ever helped at a community event?

- Have you helped to care for animals?

- Have you ever raised awareness of a good cause?

3. Discuss the lists that have been generated by the group. Invite group members to expand on what they have done and how it has had a positive impact on others. Explain how there are all sorts of things we can do to make a difference and the small things are just as important as the bigger things.

MAKING A DIFFERENCE

(14–16, 16–18)

Aim: For students to explore options for helping others in their local community.

Resources: Internet, leaflets and brochures, local library, outside speakers.

How to do it: Volunteering our time and effort has been shown to be beneficial for our happiness levels. It is thought that those who volunteer have added meaning in their lives as well as more opportunities to connect with others and feel valued. This activity is designed to help students explore some of the opportunities available in their local communities. Some might find that they discover a new hobby, interest, or gain skills which help them to gain later employment. How you deliver this activity will depend on the age and ability of your students. You might prefer to invite in speakers from local charities looking for volunteers or take students to a volunteer fair if one is taking place locally.

1. Students can work independently or in a pair to research an organisation or local opportunity for volunteer work. There are websites such as 'Do It' which advertise volunteer opportunities and some local areas have a volunteer bureau. Younger students who are not yet old enough to volunteer may like to research organisations or events which they can contribute to (e.g. the Christmas

shoebox appeal, volunteering at parkrun events with an adult, taking part in the 'Race for Life', fundraising for a national event such as 'Comic Relief').

2. Once research is complete, ask students to summarise their findings. They may like to each present to the rest of the group, or write a short summary of their cause to put together into a leaflet.

3. If a student shows a particular interest in one of the activities, support them to find out more about how to get involved. Alternatively, the whole group may decide to focus on a particular cause or event and take part as a group.

Individual activities

GRATITUDE JOURNAL

(11–14, 14–16, 16–18)

Aim: To encourage individual students to notice things that they are grateful for and things that have gone well.

Resources: A diary, notebook or planner, or an electronic version.

How to do it:

1. Explain what is meant by a 'gratitude diary', a place to note things that you are grateful for and things that have gone well. This can help to promote feelings of happiness and wellbeing as well as helping us to notice things that we would not have ordinarily focused on.

2. Ask the student to write down three things each day which they are grateful for, or that have gone well. Remind the student of all the things that this could include – people, specific things that people have done, animals, opportunities, events, acts of kindness, small things we

have noticed, ideas, general concepts. Remind students that even on bad days there are usually some things that have gone well. It is not about dismissing the negatives, but about helping ourselves to develop a more balanced view and not to let the negatives prevent us from enjoying the good things. Even 'negative' experiences can teach us things or present us with new opportunities and possibilities.

3. Once the student gets into a routine of doing this, challenge them to note down three different things each day, and not just to repeat the same ones! Also encourage students to identify what they have done well and their own part in things (e.g. 'I am getting better at not reacting immediately to my classmates' silly behaviour' or instead of 'I got good marks in a test', encourage them to recognise their personal strengths, 'I focused on my revision and got a good mark on a test').

4. Some students may want to share their gratitude diary with an adult, while others may prefer not to. Adults should respect this decision.

MAKING A DIFFERENCE

(11–14, 14–16, 16–18)

Aim: To support students to identify how they already, or could, make a difference to the lives of others.

Resources: Leaflets, brochures, websites.

How to do it: This activity is similar to the group activities 'Helping others' and 'Making a difference' but for individuals. Some students on the autism spectrum may not be particularly interested in other people. Indeed, the word 'autism' comes from the Greek word meaning 'self'. Some autistic individuals may not feel a desire to connect with other people, or others may wish to connect but feel that they do not. Some might feel lonely and isolated, or others may not feel that there is anything they can do to have a positive impact on others. This activity is designed to help students realise that they can have a positive impact on the lives of others in a number of ways.

1. Ask the student to identify any times they have made a positive difference to others. Students may like to make a list, do drawings or present this in some other way. A list of prompts is included in the 'Helping Others' group activity on page 127.

2. Some students may need support to identify these events. Remind the student that examples can be big or small, can make a difference directly or indirectly. Reflect on the list generated.

3. Next help the student to identify further opportunities they would like to explore. Perhaps there is a cause or charity they are particularly passionate about? Perhaps they enjoyed a previous experience and would like to do more of this? Use leaflets, volunteer websites or charity websites to research possible opportunities and support the student to pursue any that are of particular interest.

Adult communication
Model grateful and appreciative thinking

As with anything, children and young people learn from the people around them. Show your own gratitude and appreciation. Again, be sure not to overdo this, however, as too much 'gratitude' may appear inauthentic, unrealistic or 'fake' to some students on the autism spectrum.

Create a culture of gratitude

Whatever your role or setting, create a culture which is grateful and appreciative. Draw attention to nice things that have happened in your setting, local community or on a wider scale.

Avoid comparisons

Try to avoid making comparisons when talking about gratitude. If a child or young person on the autism spectrum is upset or annoyed about something, try not to respond with, 'You should be grateful that you have computers to use. Many children in other schools don't have this. I didn't when I was younger!', or, 'You are lucky to be able to go to football club. Lots of other people don't have this opportunity.' Comments like these won't help the individual on the autism spectrum to reduce their anxiety or frustration in that moment and may make them feel that they are not being listened to or taken seriously.

6

POSITIVE COPING

So far we have looked at how to recognise, develop and cultivate the more positive aspects of human life – developing our character strengths and promoting emotions such as happiness, optimism, hope and gratitude. We have also looked at how to support students to experience 'flow' and other positive states.

However, there are also going to be times in life which are more difficult, and this is a natural and expected part of being human. We are all going to experience emotions such as sadness, grief, disappointment, fear, anger, worry and frustration. The aim of positive psychology is not to avoid or eliminate these emotions, but to focus on coping with them effectively and positively, rather than letting them overwhelm us.

The next sections look at developing positive coping strategies. Firstly, the concept of resilience, or bouncing back, is explored, followed by the idea of developing a 'growth mindset'. There are then sections on how to improve wellbeing, and meaning and purpose.

RESILIENCE
What is resilience?

Resilience means being able to 'bounce back' from adversity. We are all likely to encounter times of stress, disappointment, loss, failure or trauma. People who are 'resilient' are able to learn from these times and move on effectively. People who are less resilient find these times harder to cope with – it might take them longer to overcome negative experiences and they might feel that they do not have the strength to bounce back.

YOUR TURN

Do you consider yourself to be a resilient person? Are there times when you have demonstrated resilience? Are there times when you have demonstrated less resilience? Do you think resilience can be learned?

Why is resilience important?

Resilience means an individual is able to restore positive mental and emotional health following a challenging or adverse situation. Resilience is important so that we do not become overwhelmed by small setbacks and to help us to cope with the ups and downs of everyday life. Being resilient has a big impact on our emotional wellbeing.

How do we become resilient?

The good news is that resilience has now been shown to be learnable and teachable (Rae 2016). It is not something that we are born with. Both adults and children can learn strategies which will help them to become more resilient. We can learn new ways of thinking and behaving which will increase our resilience, and we can also learn from previous experiences. Each individual will use different strengths, talents and tools to increase their resilience. Some examples of individual qualities which can facilitate resilience include:

- relationships with others
- humour
- inner direction/self-motivation
- independence
- optimism
- flexibility/adaptability

- love of learning

- spirituality

- self-acceptance

- communication skills.

Taking care of our wellbeing through sleep, exercise and healthy eating can also increase resilience (it is much harder to cope with negativity when we are hungry and tired!), and improving our emotional literacy can also be beneficial.

Resilience and autism

Individuals on the autism spectrum can all learn to improve their levels of resilience, just as any other individual can. We have already discussed some of the possible challenges for autistic individuals in developing resilience. Some challenges may include:

- low self-esteem

- lack of confidence in their own ability – especially if they have received a lot of support or not been expected to cope independently

- fixed thinking

- difficulties with theory of mind

- differences in how they communicate and interact with others

- literal interpretations

- difficulties in recognising and understanding feelings and emotions.

Despite these challenges, individuals on the autism spectrum can develop more resilience and a growth mindset (see the next section). Let's look at some activities to support children and young people to become more resilient.

RESILIENCE: PUTTING IT INTO PRACTICE
Group activities

PAST ACHIEVEMENTS

(7–11, 11–14, 14–16, 16–18)

Aim: For students to begin to identify their past achievements and how they have used their own resources and strengths to achieve these.

Resources: Past achievements prompts (see below).

How to do it:

1. Students create a list or poster of their achievements so far. You might like to use the list below as a prompt to support students to generate ideas. Ensure that students realise the length of their list is not important. Just a couple of examples are fine (e.g. 'I didn't used to be able to tie my shoelaces but now I can', 'I couldn't swim well but now I feel a confident swimmer'), and these can be in words or pictures.

2. Students now share their list with a supportive partner or small group. Encourage students to give their partner more detail about each of their achievements.

3. Explain to students that all of these achievements have been based on them using their personal resources and strengths. They have all shown 'resilience' to overcome challenges.

4. For older students, ask them to help their partner to identify the inner resources and strengths they used to help them be successful in each scenario. Students might benefit from referring to the strengths vocabulary introduced earlier in the book (and see Appendix D) (e.g. 'I couldn't swim well but now I feel a confident swimmer' –

their partner may help them recognise their 'perseverance' and 'determination' of continuing to go to swimming lessons every week despite finding it hard).

PAST ACHIEVEMENTS

- Something you have improved/got better at...

- Something you worked hard at...

- Something you achieved...

- Something you didn't used to be able to do but can now...

- Something you are proud of...

- A time you found difficult but got through...

- A problem that you overcame...

- Something you didn't understand but do now...

- Something you were unhappy with but now feel better about...

- Something you used to find difficult...

Examples may be school-related, related to hobbies and interests, or from students' personal, social or home lives.

WHAT IS RESILIENCE?

(11–14, 14–16, 16–18)

Aim: To help students understand what is meant by resilience.

How to do it:

1. Ask students if they have ever heard the word 'resilient'. Does anybody know what it means?

2. Explain to students that to be 'resilient' means to be able to 'bounce back' from adversity and from negative experiences. It means we do not become overwhelmed by negative experiences and give up easily, but that we

cope with the experience. We learn from the experience and use it as an opportunity to grow. An example might be of a young person who dreams of being a professional footballer. He goes along to try-outs for a local team but is not successful. A person who is not resilient may give up immediately and decide to give up football for good. A more resilient person might decide that they need to work harder during training sessions, ask for feedback and try out again a few months later.

3. Ask students to work in a small group and to see if they can identify an example of somebody being 'resilient' – this may be somebody they know, a celebrity or fictional character. Share the examples with the larger group.

4. Discuss the examples that have been identified. Explain to students that resilience is not a fixed, innate ability. Is it something that we can all learn and improve at.

LEARNING FROM MISTAKES

(7–11, 11–14, 14–16, 16–18)

Aim: To show students how mistakes can be helpful learning opportunities.

Resources: Online videos (optional).

How to do it:

1. Begin by telling students some famous examples of when 'mistakes' have actually led to new knowledge and positive outcomes. You might be able to find videos online which illustrate some of these. Some famous examples are:

    • Alexander Fleming, who discovered penicillin (which changed how many diseases and illness are treated), only came across this as he had left some petri dishes to go mouldy!

- Dr Spencer Silver was trying to create a super-adhesive glue to stick aeroplane parts together. Instead he ended up creating a super-weak adhesive and thus created the first sticky notes!

- And, according to one story, ring doughnuts were first 'invented' because the dough in the middle of doughnuts was raw, but the outside was cooked. A creative doughnut seller decided to get around the problem by simply cutting out the centre of the doughnuts and so a new trend was started!

2. Next explain to students how we learn by making mistakes – they are not something to be avoided. Sportspeople, for example, spend a lot of time practising and getting feedback from their coaches on how to improve. By getting things 'wrong' we learn what we need to do differently to make it even better. We all make mistakes all of the time – with our school work, in employment, with our friendships or in our personal lives. This is perfectly normal and is how we develop and grow as people; we are not meant to get things perfectly right the first time we do something! More important is if we learn from our mistakes.

3. Ask students if anybody would like to share an example of their own of when they have learned from a mistake. Or does anybody have any examples of famous people, sportspeople or even fictional characters who have learned from a mistake?

SUPERHEROES – FROM PROBLEMS TO CHALLENGES!

(7–11, 11–14, 14–16, 16–18)

Aim: To use fictional 'superheroes' to explore how problems or obstacles can be reframed as challenges and opportunities.

Resources: The superheroes created in Chapter 4, storyboards (written or computer generated), animation software, models – depending on the students' preferences.

How to do it:

1. If students created a 'superhero' in Chapter 4 of this book, they can use their superhero for this task. Alternatively, students may prefer to use a fictional superhero from a comic, book, film or television show.

2. Students are going to write a story for their superhero. Explain how all good stories have a 'problem' or 'obstacle' which the main character has to overcome. If the main character just gave up and said, 'It's too hard' or 'I'll never be able to solve that', then it wouldn't be a very interesting story!

3. Some students may be able to think of their own problem and storyline for their superhero to tackle. Others may need prompting. Some ideas might be:

   • The superhero loses their main superpower.

   • The superhero loses out in the 'superhero of the year' awards.

   • The superhero makes a mistake.

   • An arch-enemy deliberately puts obstacles in the superhero's way.

- The superhero is rejected by a love interest, friend or family member.

4. Students can complete the task in various ways – drawing a storyboard, making a computer animation, writing a story or cutting and sticking pictures.

5. Share the completed stories with the larger group. In the discussion, point out how the superheroes have shown resilience and which personal characteristics they put to good use.

Individual activities

DEALING WITH SETBACKS

(11–14, 14–16, 16–18)

Aim: To support the student to deal effectively with setbacks that have occurred.

Resources: Download and print Appendix I.

How to do it:

1. If a student is facing a setback, problem or obstacle, the 'Dealing with setbacks' sheet provided in Appendix I can act as a scaffold to support students to structure their thoughts and generate ideas. Focus on supporting the student, while at the same time encouraging them to generate their own solutions. Focus on the positives and the student's strengths.

LEARNING FROM SUCCESS

(7–11, 11–14, 14–16, 16–18)

Aim: To support students to learn from their successes and achievements.

How to do it: This activity is similar to the group activity 'past achievements' but designed for individuals.

1. Students create a list or poster of their achievements so far. You might like to use the list from the group activity 'Past achievements' as a prompt to support students to generate ideas.

2. Discuss with the student the personal strengths and characteristics they demonstrated to reach each of these achievements – perhaps they showed perseverance, creativity, flexibility, hard work, motivation, independence or a willingness to act on feedback.

3. Give the student a copy of their achievement list or poster to keep inside their organiser, planner, diary or a notebook. Ask the student to add to this each time they complete another 'achievement' – and remember that these can be big or small. It may be that they have learned something new, improved at something or dealt with a problem effectively. Ask the adults working with the student to draw attention to achievements which the student might not recognise by themselves.

4. This activity can be ongoing over a longer period of time. In discussion, focus on what the student has been doing to enable these things to go well.

Adult communication

Highlight how to learn from mistakes and successes

It can be equally important to show children and young people how to learn from both failures and successes. When things have gone well, encourage students to reflect on the process – what did they do which helped them to achieve and make progress? How can they remember to do more of this in the future? When things have not gone so well, encourage students to reflect on this too – What did they learn from the process? Are there elements that students will avoid or change in the future?

Support students to see criticism as constructive

It can sometimes be easy for students on the autism spectrum to interpret feedback as wholly critical, rather than constructive. Build up an atmosphere in which criticism is constructive and given at the right time with a focus on supporting the student to improve. Feedback works best when it is ongoing, rather than given just at the end of a piece of work.

GROWTH MINDSET

Growth mindset versus fixed mindset

Our mindset affects our overall sense of wellbeing and influences how we approach challenges and opportunities. The mindset that we approach life with will determine whether we see problems or challenges, setbacks or opportunities.

Research by Carol Dweck (2006) suggested that there are two types of mindset that people tend to have: a fixed mindset or a growth mindset.

> **KEY TERMS**
>
> **Fixed mindset.** In a fixed mindset we believe that our intelligence, personal qualities, skills and abilities, and those of others, are fixed and predetermined.
>
> **Growth mindset.** In a growth mindset, we believe that our skills, qualities and abilities can be improved and cultivated through effort. We believe that we, and other people, can change and grow through experience. We believe that success comes as a result of hard work, effort and perseverance.

Typical thoughts and phrases of an individual with a fixed mindset include:

- 'I'm no good at maths.'

- 'I can't do science.'

- 'I'm brilliant at history.'

- 'I give up.'

- 'I won't be able to do this.'

- 'I don't have a brain for languages.'

- 'I'll never be able to ride a bicycle.'

- 'I'll never get any better at this. I won't bother trying again.'

- 'I got really bad feedback. This obviously isn't for me.'

- 'I'll avoid that. I'll only fail anyway.'

- 'I'm good at this. I don't need to try hard.'

Typical thoughts and phrases used by individuals with a growth mindset include:

- 'I can get better at this.'

- 'I can't do this yet.'

- 'I'm still learning how to do this.'

- 'I've improved at this.'

- 'I've learned from my mistakes.'

- 'This could be a challenge.'

- 'I'm going to try hard at this.'

- 'I can try another way.'

- 'It's ok to make mistakes; that's how we learn.'

- 'I can keep trying.'

- 'I can learn from this experience.'

- 'I like a challenge.'

Mindsets are changeable. Simply by learning about the types of mindset we can begin to identify our own thought patterns and our personal reactions to challenges and learning. Individuals can also have different types of mindset in different domains. For example, we might have a fixed mindset about our ability to do maths, but adopt a growth mindset when it comes to cooking.

YOUR TURN

Would you consider yourself to have a fixed mindset or a growth mindset? Do you have different mindsets in different areas of your life?

The benefits of a growth mindset

Adopting a growth mindset can bring many advantages. A growth mindset can mean we are open to new challenges, opportunities and possibilities, whereas in a fixed mindset we tend to avoid challenges and opportunities to learn. In a growth mindset we learn from our mistakes, whereas in a fixed mindset we tend to rationalise failure. Individuals with a fixed mindset are also more likely to experience stress and feel overwhelmed by increasing pressures or changes as they believe their abilities are fixed and do not expect that they will be able to overcome challenges. Those with a fixed mindset are more likely to have low self-confidence and are more likely to give up if they do not reach their goals (Dweck 2006).

Goal setting

Having a growth mindset is also linked to the idea of goal setting. In a growth mindset we are more likely to set goals and feel that we are able to work towards them effectively. In a fixed mindset, individuals may avoid setting themselves goals, particularly ones which are new or they feel they might fail at. Some of the activities which follow focus on goal-setting techniques. There is evidence that training in goal setting increases feelings of wellbeing (MacLeod, Coates and Hetherton 2008).

GROWTH MINDSET: PUTTING IT INTO PRACTICE
Group activities

FIXED MINDSET OR GROWTH MINDSET?

(11–14, 14–16, 16–18)

Aim: To understand the difference between a growth mindset and a fixed mindset.

Resources: Download and print the 'Fixed Mindset or Growth Mindset Cards' from Appendix J (one set of cards for each pair/ small group of students).

How to do it:

1.   Begin by explaining what is meant by a 'growth mindset'. A growth mindset is when we believe we can get better at things. We believe that with effort and hard work we can improve. The opposite, a 'fixed mindset', is when we believe that our skills, abilities and intelligence are 'fixed'. We do not believe that we can get better at things.

2. Give each pair or small group small cards with the statements below. Ask them to discuss each one and make two piles – one of statements that somebody in a 'growth mindset' would use, the other that somebody in a 'fixed mindset' would use. Alternatively, read out the statements and ask students to move to one side of the room for 'growth mindset' and the other side if they think 'fixed mindset'.

3. Discuss the answers and explain why the statements indicate either a fixed or growth mindset.

FIXED MINDSET OR GROWTH MINDSET?

- I'm no good at maths.
- I can't do science.
- I'm brilliant at history.
- I give up.
- I won't be able to do this.
- I don't have a brain for languages.
- I'll never be able to ride a bicycle.
- I'll never get any better at this. I won't bother trying again.
- I got really bad feedback. This obviously isn't for me.
- I'll avoid that. I'll only fail anyway.
- I'm good at this. I don't need to try hard.

- I can get better at this.
- I can't do this yet.
- I'm still learning how to do this.
- I've improved at this.
- I've learned from my mistakes.
- This could be a challenge.
- I'm going to try hard at this.
- I can try another way.
- It's ok to make mistakes; that's how we learn.
- I can keep trying.
- I can learn from this experience.
- I like a challenge.

Mix these up before giving to students.

Answers: The *statements on the left-hand side indicate a fixed mindset; those on the right-hand side are indicative of a growth mindset.*

SUPERHERO MINDSET

(7–11, 11–14, 14–16, 16–18)

Aim: To develop further the understanding of a growth mindset through discussing situations that fictional characters find themselves in.

Resources: Superheroes from Chapter 4. Fixed and growth mindset statements from above.

How to do it: This activity has been designed as some students may find it easier to discuss problem solving and a growth mindset through using fictional characters rather than talking about themselves. Students can use the superheroes that they created in Chapter 4. Alternatively this activity can be adapted and students can discuss other fictional characters who are using a fixed or growth mindset – these may be characters from books, films or soap operas.

1. Explain that students are going to use their superheroes again to further develop their understanding of a 'growth mindset'. Alternatively students may use another superhero or fictional character (existing or of their own invention).

2. Give each student a 'growth mindset' statement from the box above. Ask them to write a story (or draw or make an animation) in which their superhero uses the growth mindset phrase and demonstrates this sort of thinking to solve a problem.

3. This activity could be adapted according to the age and interest of students: some may like to create a story in which the superhero helps somebody change from a fixed mindset way of thinking to a growth mindset way of thinking.

4. Share the completed stories with the larger group and reinforce what is meant by a growth mindset and why this is beneficial.

Individual activities

GOAL SETTING

(7–11, 11–14, 14–16, 16–18)

Aim: To support students to identify how to set goals and plan effectively.

Resources: A rating scale labelled 0–10, paper and pens.

How to do it: This activity uses a solution-focused approach to support students to set and reach their goals by developing a growth mindset.

1. Begin by exploring the positives. Ask the student what is going well in their life. What are they getting better at? What are they enjoying? Which strengths and skills do they have?

2. Now focus on the current problem or issue. Ask the student to be as specific as possible when they tell you about it. This helps the student to identify specifically what they would like to change and focus on.

3. Next discuss the student's preferred future. What is their goal, or what will it look like when this problem is solved?

4. Ask the student to use the rating scale and place themselves on a scale of 0–10 for where they currently would place themselves. Ask why they have placed themselves at that point. Even a score of 1 or 2 means that there must be some positives, otherwise they would have scored 0.

5. Ask the student what they could do to move just one step up the scale. Be specific about what needs to happen. Use the strengths and skills referred to at the beginning of the activity to support the student to identify what they have used well in the past.

6. In the next session reflect on the student's progress so far. Have they been successful? If not, do they need to adapt their next step, or do they need additional support in carrying it out? If they have been successful, what do they need to do next to move another step up the scale?

Adult communication

View challenges as opportunities

Monitor your own language and attitudes. When obstacles and problems arise for the children and young people you work with, do you automatically believe that the individual in question will not be able to overcome the barrier? Is it your natural reaction to try to remove the problem or solve it on behalf of the child or young person? Instead of seeing challenges, see opportunities and present tasks and events to students as such. Share your enthusiasm for opportunities that allow you and your students to develop and improve skills.

Focus on the process rather than the product

In some educational settings there can be an emphasis on reaching the final product (e.g. target grades, a certain level, completed pieces of work), rather than on the process of learning which is involved. In fact, it is the process which is the most important aspect of learning and this is how we learn, progress and improve – by trying things out, making mistakes and adapting what we are doing, rather than just immediately producing a finished, perfect piece of work. Value the learning process over the end result.

Mind your language

The language that we use can play a big role in developing our own mindset and that of the children and young people we are working with. This is especially important to take into consideration when working with young people on the autism spectrum who may take things very literally. For example, if a young person overhears you say that she 'can't do maths' or 'can't go into town by herself', then she may take this very literally, assuming that she, for example, will never be able to do maths, or go out independently, thus reinforcing a fixed mindset. Change the language you use:

- Use 'yet'. 'Tara is not yet able to use the past tense in French' sounds better than 'Tara can't use the past tense in French.'

- Use 'is learning'. 'You are learning how to catch a ball' is better than 'You still can't catch a ball.'

Praise effort over attainment

Praise the effort that a child or young person puts into a task, over their final attainment. It can be easy for children and young people, particularly those on the autism spectrum, to focus too much on school marks, levels and grades. For some, if they do not reach the grade they were expecting, they can automatically write off the entire subject or topic as a 'failure', without recognising the learning and development which has occurred. Others may have perfectionist tendencies, which again can be unhelpful. Whenever possible, try to highlight learning and improvements, rather than focusing on grades or levels.

WELLBEING
Wellbeing: What is it?

The word 'wellbeing' is often used and can mean different things to different people. 'Physical wellbeing' is made up of a number of components – our diet, our levels of physical activity and the quality of rest and sleep, for example. 'Emotional and mental wellbeing' often refers to how we are feeling on a general, everyday level – do we have an overall sense of being able to cope and do we generally feel positive about ourselves and our lives? The two aspects of physical and mental wellbeing are closely linked. If you have ever suffered from a lack of sleep you will know how much more difficult it is to cope when you feel exhausted! Small, everyday challenges can seem insurmountable and overtiredness can lead to a lack of energy and enthusiasm for things we would usually enjoy.

The previous chapters of this book have already covered several different aspects of emotional wellbeing, so this chapter looks predominantly at physical aspects of wellbeing and the impact that these can have on emotional wellbeing. Ideally, both aspects need to be developed and it is important not to dismiss the influence of physical wellbeing on our mental and emotional wellbeing. Sometimes this can appear a chicken-and-egg type problem. Imagine, for example, a student who has a low level of physical wellbeing. Perhaps he is chronically sleep deprived and so is exhausted during the day, being unable to concentrate and being irritable and short-tempered. Perhaps he also predominantly has sugary snacks and drinks, leading to him experiencing sudden bursts of energy followed by drops in blood sugar levels. If he also does little physical activity, he may find also that he feels lethargic and tires easily when moving about. The combination of these factors may also mean that he suffers from a negative body image and dislikes the way he looks. In this negative state he is unlikely to feel relaxed or positive enough to be able to work effectively on improving his emotional wellbeing. His constant irritability, anxiety and lethargy may also mean that he is unable to make decisions, solve problems or work towards goals. It is clear that physical wellbeing can have an impact on emotional wellbeing, and the opposite is also true. If a student is feeling constantly anxious or worried about something, then perhaps he will also be worrying about this at night and be unable to sleep. A mind whirling with thoughts will be unable to rest and relax effectively. Similarly, if we feel angry or annoyed, it can be natural to reach for sugary snacks for an instant 'fix', or if we are feeling stressed or overworked we may prioritise other tasks over physical exercise. In this section, we consider some of the possible challenges for children and young people on the autism spectrum in achieving a sense of both physical and emotional wellbeing.

Wellbeing and autism

There can sometimes be a number of challenges for children and young people on the autism spectrum in achieving a sense of physical wellbeing.

Sleep

- Sensory sensitivities can play a role – some individuals on the autism spectrum may be particularly sensitive to noise or light, or may prefer a weighted blanket.

- Anxiety and worry. Children and young people on the autism spectrum may experience a constant high level of anxiety. They might find it difficult to sleep as they are ruminating on worries and concerns.

- Unhealthy habits that impact on many children and young people will also affect those on the autism spectrum. Young people may be interrupted from sleep by their mobile devices or may be more interested in continuing their computer games rather than going to bed – screen exposure before bedtime has been shown to disrupt sleep.

Exercise

- Some young people may have been discouraged from school physical education (PE) lessons due to the emphasis on team games. Individuals on the autism spectrum can find it difficult to communicate with others during team sports and being around other people can increase their anxiety levels. Others may not feel others are tolerant when they make mistakes, or may not be tolerant of others on their team.

- Some settings may ask young people to 'pick teams'. This can be uncomfortable or embarrassing for those who are picked last.

- Instructions and rules may also be difficult to follow in team sports, especially if these are different when playing games with different groups of people.

- Motor skills can be difficult for some young people on the autism spectrum. Some might find it difficult to throw or catch a ball, to use sports equipment, or to move fluently and comfortably. Some students, therefore, may find some sports uncomfortable, or feel embarrassed exercising around others. Getting changed may also be an uncomfortable or slow process for some students.

- Sensory issues can play a role. Some students may feel uncomfortable in certain sports clothing or using certain sports equipment. Getting hot and sweaty can cause students to feel uncomfortable, particularly if there are no showers available afterwards. Those on the autism spectrum may be particularly sensitive to this.

- School PE lessons may be less structured than other lessons, which again can increase anxiety amongst autistic students.

- And all of the other issues which can discourage any young person from exercise can also be difficult for students on the autism spectrum! Body image, feeling embarrassed, not wanting to use communal changing rooms, preferring other activities, lacking confidence...these can be difficult for autistic students too.

Healthy eating

- Sensory sensitivities can impact healthy eating. Some children and young people on the autism spectrum may be particularly averse to certain tastes, smells or textures.

- Some individuals on the autism spectrum may be unwilling to try new foods, or need to eat the same meals, prepared in the same way, every day.

- For some the social nature of mealtimes can be overwhelming; others may prefer to eat in the company of family or peers (National Autistic Society 2016b).

- There is some evidence that individuals on the autism spectrum may be more likely to experience eating disorders than the rest of the population (Gillberg, Råstam and Gillberg 1995). Individuals on the autism spectrum may be particularly susceptible because of low self-esteem, high anxiety, a need to have control over their lives, a reliance on routine, interpreting language literally and fixed thinking habits. Sensory issues can also play a role, as can being particularly focused on numbers and patterns (e.g. counting calories, weight, measurements).

Other factors

In addition, there can be a number of other factors which can affect the general wellbeing level and increase anxiety in children and young people on the autism spectrum.

Sensory sensitivities

Many individuals on the autism spectrum experience sensory sensitivities; this means that they may be over- or under-sensitive to certain sensory stimuli (lights, noise, textures, tastes, smells, touch). When autistic individuals are overwhelmed by sensory input, they can experience increased anxiety, making it difficult to think and to concentrate. They may become less able to communicate and this can sometimes result in 'shutdown' (becoming extremely withdrawn and having to isolate themselves) or in 'meltdown'. Being overwhelmed by sensory input is not only extremely uncomfortable for autistic individuals, but can also be physically painful. Many everyday environments, such as schools, can be overwhelming with noises, visuals, crowds, smells and lights, so some students may find themselves in a constant state of anxiety and discomfort.

Puberty and growing up

Puberty can be a difficult time for young people on the autism spectrum. Their bodies are changing in size and shape, girls are starting their periods, and both sexes are developing feelings and emotions they have never before experienced. For young people on the autism spectrum, some of these changes can be particularly difficult to cope with.

Bullying and vulnerability

Children and young people may also be more vulnerable than others, due to their difficulties with understanding other people's perspectives and difficulties in communicating with others. They might be more likely to be bullied by others, or to interpret everyday situations as 'bullying'. Some may bully others, without realising the impact of their words or actions. Some may also be more vulnerable to peer pressure, manipulation or exploitation.

Independence

Having an appropriate level of independence is important for all young people to allow them to develop confidence and solve problems independently. Some children on the autism spectrum may feel that they lack independence compared to their peers, leading to them feeling that they have a lack of control over their life. Others may not be able to cope with the same amount of independence that their peers experience. Both extremes can cause anxiety for the individuals in question.

WELLBEING: PUTTING IT INTO PRACTICE
Group activities

WHAT CAN EXERCISE DO FOR US?

(7–11, 11–14, 14–16, 16–18)

Aim: To support students to understand the benefits of exercise and to identify forms of exercise which they might like to try out.

Resources: Pens and paper, or other recording devices, videos (optional), leaflets and brochures from local sporting facilities, list of extracurricular activities on offer.

How to do it:

1. Begin by placing students into pairs or small groups. Begin with a short 'competition'. Which team can list the most sports within the given time (try three minutes).

2. Take feedback from the group and list the sports that students named. If any sports are new to students in the group it can be helpful to show videos (available from various sources of the internet) of the different sports so that students understand what each one involves. Use the list below to add further sports and activities to the list that students may have omitted. This may also be a suitable point for members of the group to share information about the sports that they do themselves.

3. Now ask the smaller groups what the benefits of exercise are. Ask each group to make a list and then to feed back to the larger group. Some possible answers may include: to have fun, spend time with friends, spend time outdoors, keep fit, keep healthy, stronger bones and cardiovascular system, to improve mood, to relax.

4. Explain to students how there are many benefits to exercise and there are many different types of exercise – we will all prefer different things with some of us preferring team sports, or some preferring individual sports, some liking to exercise outdoors and others preferring to exercise indoors. Now give out the brochures, leaflets or lists of activities on offer in your setting and the local community. Ask students each to identify one which they might like to try out.

5. If possible in your setting, you could take a vote on which activities would be the most popular to try out, and arrange a trip or visit to the top choices.

POSSIBLE SPORTS TO NAME

Walking, jogging, running, athletics, hiking, swimming, triathlon, cycling, diving, gymnastics, going to the gym, mountain biking, roller skating, skateboarding, archery, fencing, football, rugby, volleyball, handball, tennis, badminton, squash, netball, basketball, dodgeball, hockey, dancing, yoga, pilates, aerobics, boxing, judo, karate, taekwondo, tai-chi, baseball, rounders, climbing, circuits, spinning, trampolining, weightlifting, table tennis, ice skating, skiing, snow boarding, curling, speed skating, ice hockey.

FALSE IMAGES ALL AROUND US

(7–11, 11–14, 14–16, 16–18)

Aim: For students to understand how many of the images we are exposed to are digitally manipulated and portray a false sense of reality.

Resources: Computer software which enables images to be edited. A selection of images of people and places. Digitally manipulated images.

How to do it: This activity begins by asking students to digitally manipulate an image so that they can see how easy it is to transform an image into something different. Older students can then go on to discuss why images are manipulated and the possible negative effects of this.

1. Students will need to start this activity using a computer or mobile device and will need access to computer software or apps which enable images to be digitally manipulated. Provide a starting image for students (e.g. a place, person or animal – but not a photograph of themselves or of somebody in the group) and ask them to change it how they like.

2. Once finished, present the altered images to the main group. Compare the finished products – can students see how easy it is to change an image so that it no longer represents the original?

3. Explain how many of the images we see in newspapers, magazines, online and on social media have been digitally manipulated. This is often particularly the case in advertising. Why do students think this is?

4. Explain how advertisers want to make money. They make their images look as good as they can in order to attract

people to buy the things being advertised. They may do things like make models look slimmer, change skin colour, remove spots and wrinkles, make teeth look whiter and add make-up. The finished image usually ends up looking quite different to the model in real life! Ask students to discuss the effect that this has on the audience and take some feedback from each group.

5. Now show some of the digitally manipulated images that you have found. Many of these have been edited to the extreme (arms not attached to bodies, skin a different shade on one side of the body...). Reinforce to students how many of the images we see everyday are not real but have been manipulated. It is important not to compare ourselves or our lives to these images as they do not represent reality.

USING DIGITAL TECHNOLOGIES

(11–14, 14–16)

Aim: To encourage students to use and interpret social media sites wisely and critically.

Resources: Research materials – for example, leaflets, brochures or websites about staying safe online, presentation materials – computer software or posters.

How to do it:

1. Split students into pairs or small groups. Give each pair one of the following topics: social networking sites (pros and cons), staying safe online, cyberbullying, mobile phones (pros and cons), the internet (pros and cons).

2. Students are to research their topic and summarise their findings to the rest of the group, through preparing a

computer presentation or poster (creative types may prefer to act out a role play, make a video or animation).

3. Discuss the presentations. Which issues have been brought up? How can we overcome these? Students may like to bring together their findings into a poster or leaflet designed for younger children.

THE GOOD AND THE BAD OF SOCIAL MEDIA

(11–14, 14–16, 16–18)

Aim: To explore some of the more specific difficulties that can arise from using social media, particularly those which can be of difficulty to those on the autism spectrum (but are likely to be equally as useful for others to investigate).

Resources: Large paper, sticky notes.

How to do it:

1. Write titles on two large pieces of paper: 'Good aspects of social media' and 'Bad aspects of social media'. Hang these at opposite sides of the room.

2. Ask students to work in pairs or small groups. On sticky notes they write good and bad aspects of social media and stick these on the corresponding poster.

3. Once students have finished discussing, bring the group back together for a discussion. Expand on the points made on the sticky notes.

4. Ask students if they have any examples from their own experiences which they would like to share with the class.

5. Expand this activity in various ways depending on your group – some may like to make posters, leaflets or presentations explaining how to stay safe on social media.

Other groups may need to be shown specifically how to change their privacy settings or change their newsfeed filters. Some students on the autism spectrum can have difficulty in determining when a social media user means something as a joke or seriously.

GARDENING AND THE OUTDOORS

(7–11, 11–14, 14–16, 16–18)

Aim: To increase feelings of wellbeing through spending time outdoors.

Resources: Pots, compost, seeds, outdoor space.

How to do it: Plenty of evidence shows the benefits of spending time outdoors, particularly in nature and green spaces.

1. Use an outdoor space. A small garden works well but a paved area can be just as good – many flowers and vegetables grow well in pots.

2. Provide students with pots, compost and seeds. Try growing vegetables or flowers. Some easy-to-grow vegetables include: lettuce, cress, rocket, spinach, radish, carrots, peas and herbs.

3. Water, feed and weed regularly.

4. Once fully grown, harvest, eat and enjoy!

There are plenty of other ways to increase the amount of time spent outdoors, without having to take up gardening as a hobby. Why not try some of the following?

- Trips to forests, woods, parks, nature reserves, the countryside or seaside

- Encouraging walking and cycling to school

- Arranging cycle safety lessons

- Picnics during nice weather

- Outdoor games and activities

BEING BORED

(7–11, 11–14, 14–16, 16–18)

Aim: To encourage creativity in young people

Resources: Various.

How to do it: Young people today tend to be spending more time in front of screens and television, computers and mobile devices. This means that they always have something to do. However, this has a downside, and many now feel uncomfortable when they aren't constantly connected, are unhappy in their own company and unable to entertain themselves. Many find it hard to be creative and come up with their own ideas.

1. Have times when students are not automatically provided with an activity to keep them busy. Provide a range of activities for them to choose from, but no screen-based activities. Rather than provide structured games, have a range of other materials on offer – craft materials, boxes, building materials – these all tend to work well. Leave children and young people to come up with their own entertainment!

2. Remember this activity is all about encouraging creativity – there are no right or wrong answers and do not worry if some students choose to work alone – it is all about becoming comfortable in their own company without constantly being connected to a screen. Some

younger children might need support in making choices but try not to be too prescriptive.

Individual activities

MY SENSORY PROFILE

(7–11, 11–14, 14–16, 16–18)

Aim: For students to identify their sensory preferences and strategies to cope with any sensory difficulties

Resources: Paper, coloured pens.

How to do it:

1. Explain to the student that everybody has different sensory preferences – we all have different tolerances to noise, crowds, lights, smells and tastes. However, individuals on the autism spectrum may be over- or under-sensitive to various things; this is considered to be part of the autistic differences.

2. Make headings of the different senses:

    - Sight (Visual)
    - Sound (Noises)
    - Smells
    - Tastes
    - Textures
    - Touch

3. Now ask students to list their likes and dislikes for each sense. Some may like to make lists while others will prefer to make a collage or use drawings.

4. Ask the student if any of these sensory likes or dislikes cause difficulty in their everyday life (e.g. not being able to concentrate with background noise meaning they cannot learn in class, not being able to focus under fluorescent lighting, feeling uncomfortable when others touch them).

Explain how there are things we can do to help in these sorts of situations. It may be that we need to tell other people about our preferences, we may be able to change our environment, or we might use other 'coping strategies' – these are things we can do to reduce our discomfort.

5. Work with students to identify what might work for them in each of the situations they have identified. Coping strategies and changing the environment are likely to be different for each individual. All students may benefit from making a short 'sensory profile' card outlining their needs to share with staff and other adults they work with (e.g. 'I am on the autism spectrum. This means I find it difficult to cope with some sensory input. You can help me by allowing me to work in a quiet area where there is no background noise. I also sometimes wear ear plugs to block out noises which are painful to me').

READING

(7–11, 11–14, 14–16, 16–18)

Aim: To use reading as a method of improving wellbeing, emotional literacy and empathy.

Resources: Books.

How to do it: Reading has been shown to improve wellbeing. 'Shelf-help' and 'reading on prescription' are now recognised schemes recommended by health professionals. Reading can help us to encounter characters who are similar to ourselves and helps us to realise that we are not the only ones to feel a certain way. In addition, reading allows us to get into the minds of others and so can improve our ability to empathise (Bergland 2014).

1. Encourage reading! This can be at home and at school. Provide opportunities for quiet reading and opportunities

to introduce students to new authors and books. Trips to the local library can be helpful here.

RELAXING: WHAT WORKS FOR ME?

(7–11, 11–14, 14–16, 16–18)

Aim: For students to build a personal profile of strategies that can help them to feel more relaxed and calmer.

Resources: List of relaxation strategies from below.

How to do it:

1. Ask the student to identify times when they feel frustrated, annoyed or bothered. These might be times when they feel they are unable to calm down or concentrate. Perhaps they are unable to fall asleep at night, or feel 'worked up' after certain events or encounters.

2. Explain that sometimes the best thing to do is deal with a problem (for example, if you have been unable to complete your homework it might be better to talk this through with an adult rather than lying awake worrying about it all night) but, at other times, we may simply need to engage in an activity to help our bodies and minds feel more relaxed.

3. Use the list of relaxation strategies below or create one of your own. Ask the student if they use any of these strategies already? When do they use it and how does it help? Are there any other times when it could be useful to use this strategy?

4. Now ask the student if there are any further strategies they would like to try which they feel may be helpful. Support the student to identify how to put this strategy into place.

5. During the next session ask the student to reflect on the strategy they tried. Was it helpful? Will they try this again? Are there any further strategies they would like to try?

6. Some students might benefit from making a small visual reminder, such as a small poster or bookmark, of relaxation strategies they find helpful.

Some possible relaxation strategies can include:

- Listening to music

- Colouring in

- Concentrating on breathing slowly

- Reading a book

- Drawing

- Walking

- Doing exercise

- Having a bath

- Visualising a calm and special place

- Spending time with your pet

KEEPING A JOURNAL

(11–14, 14–16, 16–18)

Aim: To learn how to manage feelings and emotions through journalling.

Resources: A notepad, journal, diary or scrapbook (or electronic version if preferred).

How to do it: Keeping a journal has been proven to have a therapeutic effect and can help individuals to recognise, understand and manage their feelings and emotions as well as reflect on events and record the positives (see 'Wellbeing' earlier in this chapter for more detailed information).

1. If the student is interested in keeping a journal, provide them with a notepad, journal, or other form that appeals to them. Remind them that there are no rules when it comes to keeping a journal!

    • They can write as much or as little as they like.

    • They can write as often or as little as they like.

    • It does not have to be complete sentences and spelling does not have to be correct!

    • There can be a mixture of words, pictures, drawings, photos, captions, diagrams or collages.

    • They can write about things they have enjoyed and things that have gone well.

    • They can write about things that have happened to help them make sense of them.

    • They can write about their worries and frustrations.

    • A journal is a bit like a friend – you can be honest with it and it will not judge you. It can help you to reflect and feel better about things.

    • They do not have to show their journal to anybody else, unless they feel it would be helpful to share it with a trusted adult. A journal is private and allows us to express ourselves without fear of other people's judgements.

Adult communication

Listen to 'student voice'

Ensure that students on the autism spectrum are included when your setting collects the opinions of students. Ask students to reflect on what impacts on their wellbeing in your school or college (both positively and negatively). They might highlight issues that staff had not previously considered.

Avoid categorising food as 'good' and 'bad'

In schools and educational settings there has been a recent emphasis on encouraging healthy eating, in order to combat the growing crisis of obesity. However, the way in which some of these programmes are presented and delivered may not be appropriate for some students on the autism spectrum. Be aware of categorising food into 'good' and 'bad', or into 'healthy' and 'unhealthy'. Some students on the autism spectrum can take these categories very literally and it may lead to some individuals eliminating entire food groups from their diet and narrowing their food choices. Individuals on the autism spectrum have been shown to have an increased risk of experiencing eating disorders (Shea 2016) and one of the contributing factors may be this tendency for black-and-white, literal thinking. So make sure that you are not encouraging students to see foods as 'good' or 'bad' but, instead, focus on the fact that we need lots of different types of food for our bodies, but that some of these our bodies need less of than others.

Consider the language you use about food and body image

Many adults spend a lot of time talking about diets, their weight and body image – you only have to look at the front covers of popular magazines to see that this has become an engrained part of our culture. The constant exposure to these attitudes can be difficult for all young people, particularly girls, who then grow up with these attitudes themselves. Children and young people on the autism spectrum can be particularly vulnerable to experiencing eating disorders and negative body image due to interpreting things very literally. So, mind the language that you use about food and body image when you are around children and young people on the autism spectrum:

- 'I'm being good today. I've brought salad for lunch', 'I shouldn't have a biscuit, it's very naughty' – language such as this can be interpreted literally by students on the autism spectrum who may then begin to associate eating healthily with 'being a good person' and that making unhealthy food choices makes them a bad, or 'naughty' person.

- 'You look good. Have you lost weight?' – If the first thing that you comment on is somebody's weight, then consider the message you are giving out to young people around you. They may then associate 'looking good' with 'losing weight'.

- 'She's put on weight' – If students hear you comment negatively about others, whether real-life acquaintances or celebrities in magazines, then they too will absorb these attitudes and begin to associate gaining weight as being undesirable.

Model healthy behaviours

Children and young people, whether on the autism spectrum or not, all learn from the behaviour they see demonstrated by the adults around them. If they see adults who are constantly 'on a diet', skipping meals and counting calories, then they will see this as normal behaviour. Be aware of the messages you are giving through your own behaviour and attitudes.

The sensory environment

Schools and other institutions are often large and overwhelming places for autistic children and young people. Each individual will have different sensory preferences and tolerances, so one of the best things that adults can do is to get to know the individuals they are working with. In addition, it is well worth auditing the physical environment and making some general changes which will benefit a number of students, helping to reduce anxiety and increase wellbeing. A checklist is included below.

Environmental sensory checklist

- Is natural light used where possible? Fluorescent lighting can be particularly uncomfortable for some autistic students, so when possible turn lights off and open curtains or blinds. Lights which have a 'dimmer' setting may also be useful.

- Is background noise eliminated where possible? Consider noise from outside and from neighbouring classrooms.

- Are there any uncomfortable sounds within the classroom? Humming from computer monitors and projectors can be amplified for autistic students. Turn them off when not in use.

- Does just one person talk at a time? Some autistic individuals can find it difficult to concentrate on one person talking if other people in the room are talking at the same time. Two adults whispering at the back of the classroom can be enough to mean that some students are unable to concentrate. Having additional adults repeating and rephrasing things while the main teacher is talking can also be confusing.

- Are quiet spaces available? Some autistic students will need to make use of quiet spaces. They may be more able to concentrate if they are able to work in a quiet area, so ensure that there are quiet work spaces around the school which are easily accessible and students are able to make use of.

- Is the room well organised? Rooms which look 'messy' may increase anxiety for some autistic students as this can be distracting. Store resources and materials tidily in cupboards or on shelves and label resources, cupboards and trays consistently so that students are able to find equipment easily.

- Are displays clear and helpful? Some students may also be easily distracted by overwhelming visuals and may be unable to eliminate unnecessary information. Keep displays clear, useful and tidy. Check that the information is necessary and remove anything that is unhelpful.

- Does signage support students to navigate the setting? Support students by labelling different areas, rooms and resources clearly. Use pictures and symbols to support written instructions and information. Ensure that important information is at eye level for students.

- Are social times supported? Some students on the autism spectrum will prefer to spend break and lunchtimes alone in a quiet area; the interaction during lessons can be enough for them and they need time alone to relax and 'recover' from this, so ensure that there are quiet areas available which they can use. Others may want to join in with their peers but may find this difficult. They might benefit from being able to participate in more structured activities such as a computer club, watching a film, organised games or art club.

- Is there consistency? Consistency and routine can also help to reduce anxiety for students on the autism spectrum. Clear and consistent rules across all lessons and staff will help, and explain to students why rules are in place. A well-structured day, supported by referring to visual timetables and plans, will also be beneficial.

MEANING AND PURPOSE

What is meant by 'meaning and purpose'?

YOUR TURN

What brings you meaning and purpose in your life?

Did you find it difficult to answer the previous question? You won't be alone if you did! Philosophers have been debating the meaning of life for centuries and few people take time to consider the question in-depth while going through their everyday lives.

Is having meaning and purpose important?

Evidence shows that having a sense of meaning and purpose in our lives has many wellbeing benefits and helps us to cope in tough times (King 2017). Meaning and purpose have been associated with a number of positive outcomes including subjective wellbeing, health, longevity, reduced stress and resilience (LeBon 2014).

Does searching for meaning and purpose have downsides?

Although having meaning and purpose in our lives is generally associated with positive outcomes, it is less certain if the *search* for meaning and purpose increases wellbeing. Some researchers suggest that deliberately searching for meaning in our lives may be less beneficial (Yalom 1989), for example, by increasing anxiety, over-thinking and rumination (LeBon 2014).

How do we find meaning and purpose?

What is meaningful is different for all of us. Experts generally identify four common sources of meaning (Esfahani Smith 2017):

- A sense of belonging (our relationships with others).

- Purpose (a feeling of contributing to the world).

- Storytelling (how we make sense of the world around us).

- Transcendence (connecting with something bigger than ourselves).

Values

Identifying our personal values can help us to seek out opportunities which are meaningful to us. When discussing values with young people it is important that they feel able to express their individuality and are not influenced by peer pressure or choosing things because everybody else does. Research indicates that values need to be owned by the individual in order for them to contribute to a feeling of meaning and purpose (Deci and Ryan 1985). It is important for the individual to identify with them on a personal level rather than choosing 'values' because the people around them have.

Meaning, purpose and autism

Identifying meaning and purpose can be just as difficult for individuals on the autism spectrum as for anybody else. Indeed it may be more difficult, due to lacking a sense of belonging and connection with others and living in a world which has not been designed for their way of thinking. However, many individuals on the autism spectrum do go on to find meaning and purpose in their lives.

MEANING AND PURPOSE: PUTTING IT INTO PRACTICE

As mentioned above, directly searching for meaning and purpose may not always necessarily lead to positive outcomes. This is not something that can be directly taught, or not something that it is always beneficial to focus on too much. There are, therefore, fewer activities in this section; they do not directly teach 'meaning and purpose' but are designed to create opportunities for young people to discover what is meaningful to them. The following activities can be used with either groups or individuals.

Activities

WHAT IS IMPORTANT TO YOU? VALUES CLARIFIER

(14–16, 16–18)

Aim: To support the student to identify and clarify the values that are important to them.

Resources: Paper, pens, computer software; yearbooks, photos or other visuals made in previous activities, if available; download and print Appendix K.

How to do it:

1. Using the student's preferred method (e.g. spider diagram, collage, computer presentation, drawing, poster, model, list) ask them to create a poster titled 'What is important to me?' Encourage them to be as creative as they like. This can then be used to facilitate discussion about activities they might benefit from getting involved in, or to support future lifestyle and career choices.

2. Many students will find it easier to identify things (my cat, playing on computer games, my friends...) rather than concepts (e.g. friendship, community, looking after the environment, autonomy...). Considering the wider 'concepts' or 'values' can support students to seek out new opportunities and to recognise why they enjoy some tasks more than others. To support students in extending their lists you could try some of the following:

   • Ask your student to make a comic strip of an ideal day – it can be a really good day that has happened, or their ideal day. Include details in the comic strip of what you did, which activities you engaged with, things that people said, places you went to. Discuss what made (would make) this a good day. This can suggest what brings the student meaning and what they value.

- Ask your student to identify a reaction they were proud of. When have they responded to an event in a way they felt good about? Again, this might suggest some of the values which are meaningful to the student.

- Who do you admire? Ask the student to identify people they admire – these may be famous people, people in their families, peers or other role models. They might like to draw these people or find photos of them. Why do they admire each one? Try to pull out specific examples – this may indicate values that are important to the student.

- (This may be a bit morbid for some students, but others can find it useful.) Ask the student, if they had only a few months left to live, what would they do? How would they fill their time? What would they want to complete? Alternatively, use the 'bucket list' exercise – what would the student like to achieve in their lifetime? This can highlight their values.

- Finally, some students may like to read the values list (Appendix K) and identify which are meaningful to them.

3. A combination of these activities will enable most students to identify their values. Remember to point out that values are not fixed. As we grow older and have new experiences our values can change. Understanding our values, or what motivates us, can be useful self-knowledge and can help us to make decisions.

CAREERS COACHING

(14–16, 16–18)

Aim: To support students on the autism spectrum to make career choices that are meaningful to them.

Resources: Internet; pens and paper; meeting with careers advisor; leaflets, brochures and books from local colleges, universities, employers, volunteer organisations, career services and work schemes (depending on student's age and interests).

How to do it: Making decisions can be difficult for any young person. Which subjects to study at school or college? Whether or not to go to university? What sort of job or career they would like to pursue? Young people on the autism spectrum can have additional difficulties – they might lack self-esteem or self-knowledge or worry that they will not be able to do some jobs. Even just applying for a job or surviving an interview can be difficult for many due to differences in the way they communicate. Many young people make the mistake of having an 'outside-in' approach to a job – they see a job and decide they would like to do that job, although it may not be suited to their particular strengths and values. Better is to use an 'inside-out' approach to encourage the young person to identify what is important to them and then identify jobs which will enable them to use these skills and values.

1. Before looking into careers, learn how to ask the right questions to identify what really matters to the student. Try some of the following:

    • What are you good at? (skills, strengths, talents...)

    • What makes you feel energised and happy?

    • What is important to you?/What are your values?

    • What drains your energy?

- What does work mean to you?

- What sort of physical environment would you like to work in?

- What lifestyle do you want to be living? (e.g. would you consider shift work, working from home, self-employment?)

2. Next consider the impact the student's autism may have. Try asking some of the following:

- What differences do you have in the way you communicate? How might this affect what job you do?

- Do you have any sensory differences?

- Would you be willing to wear a uniform?

- Do you prefer working independently or in a team? Do you like being around others and for how long?

- How easy do you find it to plan and organise your time?

- How do you cope with changes of routine?

3. Provide opportunities for students to find out about jobs and careers as there may be many they have not previously considered. Career fairs can be useful, as can using websites aimed at young people which give information about a range of jobs.

4. Support the young person to try out different jobs. This may begin with shadowing a parent, relative or neighbour for a short time to experience the workplace. Students may move on to completing work experience more independently, doing volunteer work or having a holiday or weekend job. Encourage students to reflect on their experiences, good or bad. What did they enjoy? What would they like to find out more about? What did they not like?

Adult communication

Encourage a sense of belonging

A sense of belonging is important for many people to feel a sense of meaning and purpose in their lives. Ensure that autistic students have an accepting environment in the school setting and feel valued. Also encourage students to 'find their tribe', people who accept them, have similar interests and who motivate them. Are there extracurricular activities available in school? What is going on in the community? It is only in school that we expect students to socialise with people exactly the same age as them, so do not be restricted by this – having slightly older or younger friends is not a problem if the friendship group is supportive and caring.

Encourage individuality

As an adult working with students on the autism spectrum, self-awareness is vital. Try not to impose your own values on to the young person, and be aware if the young person is simply saying what they think they ought to say (e.g. what is considered 'acceptable') rather than what is truly meaningful to them.

GLOSSARY

ALNCO Additional learning needs co-ordinator. Another term for 'SENCO'.

ASPERGER SYNDROME An autism spectrum condition which referred to individuals who were on the autism spectrum and had no co-occurring learning difficulties. Individuals with this profile are now given a diagnosis of 'Autism Spectrum Disorder Level 1'.

BIBLIOTHERAPY The use of books as treatment for various mental or physical conditions.

BROADEN AND BUILD THEORY A theory proposed by psychologist Barbara Fredrickson about the importance of positive emotions. Positive emotions lead to a broadened mindset which leads you to build personal resources such as psychological strengths. These in turn make it more likely that you have more positive experiences and increase your wellbeing.

DSM-5 The fifth edition of the Diagnostic and Statistical Manual of the American Psychiatric Association, often used to define and diagnose autism.

EMOTIONAL INTELLIGENCE The ability to recognise and understand our own and other people's emotions, manage these effectively and to handle interpersonal relationships empathetically.

EMOTIONAL LITERACY A term used to describe the ability to understand and express our feelings and emotions.

FIXED MINDSET In a fixed mindset you believe that your intelligence, personal qualities and abilities are fixed and won't grow or develop over time.

FLOURISHING A term coined by Martin Seligman to replace 'happiness' which he considers to be over-used and meaningless. 'Flourishing' implies that an individual has meaning and purpose in their lives, is fulfilling their potential, making positive use of their strengths, and is connected to some wider connection or purpose.

FLOW A state identified by psychologist Mikhail Csikszentmihalyi, in which the individual experiences a state of total engagement with the activity.

GROWTH MINDSET A state of mind identified by American psychologist Carol Dweck. In a fixed mindset an individual believes that their intelligence and abilities are fixed; in a growth mindset, an individual believes they can increase their intelligence and abilities with determination and hard work.

HFA (HIGH FUNCTIONING AUTISM) Another term formerly used to describe individuals on the autism spectrum who did not have learning difficulties. Individuals now receive a diagnosis of 'Autism Spectrum Disorder Level 1'.

NEGATIVITY BIAS The tendency to focus on negative things, people and events more than the positive.

NEURODIVERSITY The diversity, or variation, of ways in which humans think, learn and relate to others. This diversity is seen as a normal, and expected, part of human variation.

PDA (PATHOLOGICAL DEMAND AVOIDANCE) PDA is now seen as being part of the autism spectrum. Individuals who have a diagnosis of PDA will avoid demands made by others due to high levels of anxiety.

PDD-NOS (PERVASIVE DEVELOPMENTAL DISORDER – NOT OTHERWISE SPECIFIED) Diagnosis given to individuals who may have met some, but not all, of the autistic traits.

POSITIVE PSYCHOLOGY A branch of psychology which has grown in popularity since the beginning of the twenty-first century. Positive psychology investigates how to increase and enhance the positive aspects of human existence (positive emotions, resilience, happiness and wellbeing...) rather than traditional psychology which attempts to remediate deficits.

POSITIVE REMINISCENCE Recalling and reliving positive and happy memories. This has been shown to boost feelings of wellbeing.

PROPRIOCEPTION The ability to be aware of the position of one's body in space (often a difficulty for some individuals on the autism spectrum).

SAVOURING Deliberately attending to and appreciating positive experiences. Using all of the senses to become immersed and really enjoy what is going on.

SENCO Special educational needs co-ordinator. Each school in the UK will have a SENCO who should be your first point of contact if you have concerns about a child with possible special educational needs, including autism.

SIGNATURE STRENGTHS An individual's top strengths; when they use these they feel energised and invigorated.

SUBJECTIVE WELLBEING (SWB) Term often used by positive psychologists to overcome the vagueness and ambiguity of the word 'happiness'.

THEORY OF MIND (TOM) The ability to understand that other people have thoughts, feelings, knowledge and perceptions different to one's own; often considered to be a difficulty for individuals on the autism spectrum.

REFERENCES

American Psychiatric Association (2013) *Diagnostic and Statistical Manual of Mental Disorders, 5th edition*, DSM-5. Washington, DC: American Psychiatric Association.

Attwood, T. (2007) *The Complete Guide to Asperger Syndrome.* London: Jessica Kingsley Publishers.

Bergland, C. (2014) 'Can reading a fictional story make you more empathetic?' *Psychology Today*, 1 Dec. Accessed on 19/06/2017 at https://psychologytoday.com/blog/the-athletes-way/201412/can-reading-fictional-story-make-you-more-empathetic.

Billstedt, E., Gillberg, C. and Gillberg, C. (2011) 'Aspects of quality of life in adults diagnosed with autism in childhood: A population based study.' *Autism 15*, 1, 7–20. Accessed on 19/06/2017 at www.gnc.gu.se/digitalAssets/1349/1349896_billstedt-aspects-of-quality-of-life.pdf.

Boniwell, I. (2008) *Positive Psychology in a Nutshell* (2nd edn). London: PWBC.

Boniwell, I. (2015) 'Setting them up for a happy future.' *Psychologies Magazine*, August.

Boniwell, I. and Ryan, L. (2012) *Personal Well-Being Lessons for Secondary Schools: Positive Psychology in Action.* Milton Keynes: Open University Press.

Burkeman, O. (2017) 'A good talking-to.' *Psychologies Magazine*, May, 17.

Clifton, D. and Anderson, E. (2001) *StrengthsQuest.* Washington, DC: Gallup Organisation.

Connor, T.S., DeYoung, C.G. and Silvia, P.J. (2016) 'Everyday creative activity as a path to flourishing.' *Journal of Positive Psychology*. Published online 17/11/2016. Accessed on 04/07/2017 at http://www.tandfonline.com/doi/full/10.1080/17439760.2016.1257049.

Csikszentmihalyi, M. (1992) *Flow: The Psychology of Happiness.* London: Rider.

Danner, D., Snowdon, D. and Friedsen, W. (2001) 'Positive emotions early in life and the longevity: findings from the nun study.' *Journal of Personality and Social Psychology 80*, 5, 804–813.

Deci, E.L. and Ryan, R.M. (1985) *Intrinsic Motivation and Self-Determination in Human Behaviour.* New York: Plenum.

Diebel, T. (2014) 'The Effectiveness of a Gratitude Diary Intervention on Primary School Children's Sense of School Belonging.' Doctoral thesis, University of Southampton. Accessed on 19/06/2017 at https://eprints.soton.ac.uk/371951.

Dweck, C. (2006) *Mindset: The New Psychology of Success.* New York: Balantine Books.

Easterlin, R. (2008) 'Income and happiness: Towards a unified theory.' *The Economic Journal 11*, 473, 465–484.

Emmons, R. (2007) *Thanks! How the New Science of Gratitude Can Make You Happier.* New York: Houghton-Mifflin.

Esfahani Smith, E. (2017) *The Power of Meaning: Crafting a Life That Matters.* New York: Crown Publishing.

Fox Eades, J. (2008) *Celebrating Strengths: Building Strengths-Based Schools.* Coventry: CAPP Press.

Fredrickson, B. (2001) 'The role of positive emotions in positive psychology: The broaden-and-build theory of positive emotions.' *American Psychologist 56,* 3, 218–226.

Fredrickson, B. (2009) *Positivity.* New York: Crown Publishers.

Fredrickson, B.L., Mancuso, R.A, Branigan, C. and Tugade, M.M. (2000) 'The undoing effect of positive emotions.' *Motivation and Emotion 24,* 4, 237–258.

Gillberg, I.C., Råstam, M. and Gillberg, C. (1995) 'Anorexia nervosa 6 years after onset.' *Comprehensive Psychiatry 36,* 1, 61–69.

Gould, J. and Ashton-Smith, J. (2011) 'Missed diagnosis or misdiagnosis? Girls and women on the autism spectrum.' *Good Autism Practice Journal 12,* 1, 34–41.

Govindji, R. and Linley, P.A. (2007) 'Strengths use, self-concordance and well-being: Implications for strengths coaching and coaching psychologists.' *International Coaching Psychology Review 2,* 2, 143–153.

Gray, C. (2015) *The New Social Story Book.* Arlington, TX: Future Horizons.

Hurley, E. (2014) *Ultraviolet Voices: Stories of Women on the Autism Spectrum.* Birmingham: Autism West Midlands.

Ifcher, J. and Zarghamee, H. (2011) 'Positive affect and overconfidence: A laboratory investigation.' SCU Leavey School of Buisness Research Paper No. 11-02. Accessed on 19/06/2017 at http://ssrn.com/abstract=1740013.

Jamison, T.R. and Schuttler, J.O. (2015) 'Examining social competence, self-perception, quality of life and internalising and externalising symptoms in adolescent females with and without autism spectrum disorders: A quantitative design including between-groups and correlational analyses.' *Molecular Autism 17,* 6, 6–53.

Judge, T.A. and Hurst, C. (2007) 'Capitalising on one's advantage: Role of core self-evaluations.' *Journal of Applied Psychology 92,* 5, 1212–1227.

Khanna, R., Jariwala-Parikh, K., West-Strum, D. and Mahabaleshwarkar, R. (2014) 'Health related quality of life and its determinants among adults with autism.' *Research in Autism Spectrum Disorders 8,* 3, 157–167.

Kim, J.A., Szatmari, P., Bryson, S., Streiner, D.L. and Wilson, F. (2000) 'The prevalence of anxiety and mood problems among children with autism and Asperger Syndrome.' *Autism: The International Journal of Research and Practice 4,* 2, 117–132.

King, V. (2015) 'Why goals make us happy.' *Psychologies Magazine,* August.

King, V. (2017) 'Meaning mindset.' *Psychologies Magazine,* June, 130.

Kutscher, M. (2016) *Digital Kids: How to Balance Screen Time and Why It Matters.* London: Jessica Kingsley Publishers.

Kuzmanovic, B., Rigoux, L. and Vogeley, K. (2016) 'Brief report: Reduced optimism bias in self-referential belief updating in high functioning autism.' *Journal of Autism and Developmental Disorders*, 18 October. Accessed on 19/06/2017 at www.researchgate.net/publication/309270388_Brief_Report_Reduced_Optimism_Bias_in_Self-Referential_Belief_Updating_in_High-Functioning_Autism.

LeBon, T. (2014) *Achieve Your Potential through Positive Psychology.* London: Hodder and Stoughton.

Linley, P.A. (2008) *From Average to A+.* Warwick: CAPP Press.

Linley, P.A., Nielsen, K.M., Wood, K.M., Gillett, R. and Biswas-Diener, R. (2010) 'Using signature strengths in pursuit of goals: Effects on goal progress, need satisfaction and well-being, and implications for coaching psychologists.' *International Coaching Psychology Review 5*, 1, 8–17.

Lyubomirsky, S. (2007) *The How of Happiness.* London: Sphere.

Lyubomirsky, S., King, L. and Diener, E. (2005) 'The benefits of frequent positive affect: Does happiness lead to success?' *Psychological Bulletin 131*, 6, 803–855.

Lyubomirsky, S., Sheldon, K.M. and Schkade, D. (2005) 'Pursuing happiness: The architecture of sustainable change.' *Review of General Psychology 9*, 2, 111–131.

MacLeod, A.K., Coates, E. and Hetherton, J. (2008) 'Increasing well-being through teaching goal-setting and planning skills: Results of a brief intervention.' *Journal of Happiness Studies 9*, 2, 185–196.

McDonell, A. and Milton, D. (2014) 'Going with the flow: Reconsidering repetitive behaviour through the concept of flow states.' *Good Autism Practice Journal: Happiness, Autism and Wellbeing*, September, 38–47.

Minhas, G. (2010) 'Developing realised and unrealised strengths: Implications for engagement, self-esteem, life satisfaction and well-being.' *Assessment and Development Matters 2*, 1, 12–16.

National Autistic Society (2016a) 'Autism: What Is Autism?' Accessed on 19/06/2017 at www.autism.org.uk/about/what-is/asd.aspx.

National Autistic Society (2016b) 'Eating.' Accessed on 19/06/2017 at www.autism.org.uk/about/health/eating.aspx.

Office for National Statistics (2016) 'Measuring national wellbeing – at what age is personal wellbeing the highest?' Accessed on 19/06/2017 at www.ons.gov.uk/peoplepopulationandcommunity/wellbeing/articles/measuringnational wellbeing/atwhatageispersonalwellbeingthehighest.

Park, N. and Peterson, C. (2006) 'Moral competence and character strengths among adolescents: The development and validation of the Values in Action Inventory of Strengths for Youth.' *Journal of Adolescence 29*, 6, 891–909.

Peterson, C. and Park, N. (2003) 'Positive psychology as the even-handed positive psychologist views it.' *Psychological Enquiry 14*, 2, 115–120.

Rae, T. (2016) *The Wellbeing Toolkit.* London: Nurture Group Network

Rae, T. and MacConville, R. (2015) *Using Positive Psychology to Enhance Student Achievement: A Schools-Based Programme for Character Education.* Abingdon: Routledge.

Renty, J. and Royers, H. (2006) 'Satisfaction with formal support and education for children with autism spectrum disorder: The voices of the parents.' *Child Care and Health Development 32*, 3, 371–385.

Rowe, A. (2015) *The Memes Book.* CreateSpace.

Seligman, M. (2002) *Authentic Happiness.* New York: Free Press.

Seligman, M. (2011) *Flourish: A New Understanding of Happiness and Well-Being and How to Achieve Them.* London: Nicholas Brearley Publishing.

Seligman, M. and Csikszentmihalyi, M. (2000) 'Positive psychology: An introduction.' *American Psychologist 55*, 1, 5–14.

Seligman, M., Steen, T., Park, N. and Peterson, P. (2005) 'Positive psychology progress: Empirical validation of interventions.' *American Psychologist 60*, 5, 410–421.

Shea, E. (2016) 'Eating disorder or disordered eating? Eating patterns in autism.' Network Autism, 24 May. Accessed on 04/07/2017 at http://network.autism.org.uk/good-practice/case-studies/eating-disorder-or-disordered-eating-eating-patterns-autism.

Simone, R. (2010) *Aspergirls: Empowering Females with Asperger Syndrome.* London: Jessica Kingsley Publishers.

Snyder, C.R. (2000) *Handbook of Hope.* Orlando, FL: Academic Press.

Solomon, M., Miller, M., Taylor, S.L., Hinshaw, S. and Carter, C.S. (2012) 'Autism symptoms and internalising psychopathology in girls and boys with autism spectrum disorders.' *Journal of Autism and Developmental Disorders 42*, 1, 48–59.

Van Heijst, B. and Geurts, H. (2014) 'Quality of life in autism across the lifespan: A meta-analysis.' *Autism 19*, 2, 158–167.

Van Wijngaarden-Cremers, P.J., Van Eeten, E., Groen, W.B., Van Deurzen, P.A., Oosterling, I.J. and Van der Gaag, R.J. (2014) 'Gender and age differences in the core triad of impairments in autism spectrum disorders: A systematic review and meta-analysis.' *Journal of Autism and Developmental Disorders 44*, 3, 627–635.

Vermeulen, P. (2014) 'The practice of promoting happiness in autism.' *Good Autism Practice Journal: Autism, Happiness and Wellbeing,* September.

Vermeulen, P. (2016) 'Promoting happiness in autistic people.' Network Autism, 18 May. Accessed on 19/06/2017 at http://network.autism.org.uk/knowledge/insight-opinion/promoting-happiness-autistic-people.

Weldon, J. (2014) *Can I Tell You about Autism? A Guide for Friends, Family and Professionals.* London: Jessica Kingsley Publishing.

Wilson, T.D. (2011) *Redirect: The Surprising New Science of Psychological Change.* London: Allen Lane.

Yalom, I. (1989) *Love's Executioner.* London: Penguin.

Young, R. (2009) *Asperger Syndrome Pocketbook.* Alresford: Teachers' Pocketbooks.

FURTHER READING AND RESOURCES

POSITIVE PSYCHOLOGY

Boniwell, I. (2008) *Positive Psychology in a Nutshell*. London: PWBC.

Carr, A. (2004) *Positive Psychology*. Hove: Brunner-Routledge.

Csikszentmihalyi, M. (1992) *Flow: The Psychology of Happiness*. London: Rider.

Peterson, C. and Seligman, M. (2004) *Character Strengths and Virtues: A Handbook and Classification*. New York: Oxford University Press.

Snyder, C.R. and Lopez, S.J. (2002) *Handbook of Positive Psychology*. New York: Oxford University Press.

POSITIVE PSYCHOLOGY ORGANISATIONS

European Network for Positive Psychology (ENPP)

www.enpp.eu

International Positive Psychology Association (IPPA)

www.ippanetwork.org

Personal Wellbeing Centre

www.personalwellbeingcentre.org

Positive Psychology Center, University of Pennsylvania

www.ppc.sas.upenn.edu

Positive Psychology UK

http://positivepsychology.org.uk

University of Cambridge Well-being Institute

www.wellbeing.group.cam.ac.uk

AUTISM

Attwood, T. (2007) *The Complete Guide to Asperger Syndrome.* London: Jessica Kingsley Publishers.

Baron-Cohen, S. (2008) *The Facts: Autism and Asperger Syndrome.* Oxford: Oxford University Press.

Honeybourne, V. (2016) *Educating and Supporting Girls with Asperger's and Autism.* London: Speechmark.

Sainsbury, C. (2009) *Martian in the Playground: Understanding the Schoolchild with Asperger's Syndrome.* London: Sage.

Schlegelmilch, A. (2014) *Parenting ASD Teens.* London: Jessica Kingsley Publishers.

Vermeulen, P. (2012) *Autism as Context Blindness.* Kansas: AAPC.

Welton, J. (2014) *Can I Tell You about autism? A Guide for Friends, Family and Professionals.* London: Jessica Kingsley Publishers.

Willey, L.H. (2015) *Pretending to be Normal: Living with Asperger Syndrome* (2nd edn). London: Jessica Kingsley Publishers.

Winter, M. and Lawrence, C. (2011) *Asperger Syndrome: What Teachers Need to Know.* London: Jessica Kingsley Publishers.

Young, R. (2009, reprinted 2011) *Asperger Syndrome Pocketbook.* Alresford: Teachers' Pocketbooks.

AUTISM SUPPORT ORGANISATIONS

Ambitious About Autism

www.ambitiousaboutautism.org.uk

American Asperger's Association

http://americanaspergers.forumotion.net

Asperger Syndrome Foundation

www.aspergerfoundation.org.uk

Autism Education Trust

www.autismeducationtrust.org.uk

Autism New Zealand

www.autismnz.org.nz

Autism Society Canada

www.autismcanada.org

Autism Spectrum Australia

www.autismspectrum.org.au

Autism West Midlands

www.autismwestmidlands.org.uk

National Autistic Society

www.autism.org.uk

The Den

www.theden.me

US Autism and Asperger Association

www.usautism.org

CHILDREN AND YOUNG PEOPLE'S MENTAL HEALTH

HeadMeds – information aimed at young people about medication

www.headmeds.org.uk

MindEd – online, free training modules for both professionals and parents in all aspects of mental and emotional wellbeing

www.minded.org.uk

Young Minds – information about young people's mental health

https://youngminds.org.uk

APPENDICES

The Appendices are available to download and print from www.jkp.com/voucher using the code HONEYBOURNEHAPPINESS.

Appendix A

STRENGTHS AND DEFINITIONS CARDS

STRENGTHS CARDS

Creativity	Optimism	Adaptability
Perseverance	Gratitude	Enthusiasm
Self-control	Open-mindedness	Kindness

Responsibility	**Forgiveness**	**Reliability**
Leadership	**Honesty**	**Fairness**
Curiosity	**Sociability**	**Love of learning**
Teamwork	**Independence**	**Generosity**
Humour	**Spirituality**	**Equality**

Emotional intelligence	**Critical thinking**	**Modesty**
Patience	**Organisation**	**Authenticity**

DEFINITIONS CARDS

Being original and finding new ways of doing things	Being hopeful and looking for positive things	Being flexible and able to adjust to different circumstances
Keeping on trying even though things may be difficult or you face setbacks	Being thankful for good things in your life and positive things that happen	Doing things with energy, eagerness and passion

Controlling your thinking and behaviour when it is necessary

Respecting and considering other people's opinions and points of view; not jumping to conclusions or prejudices

Doing nice things for other people, caring and looking out for others

Being trusted to do something and knowing the difference between right and wrong

Excusing people when they have made a mistake and giving them a second chance

You can be trusted to do what you say you will do

Directing and organising tasks or events and encouraging others to join in

Telling the truth

Giving everybody an equal chance, regardless of your personal opinions

Being interested in new things and asking questions

Getting on well with others in social situations

Enjoying learning new knowledge and finding out new things

Working well within a group of people

Being able to do things by yourself

Sharing your time, belongings or effort with others

Being able to see the funny side of things

Believing in something 'bigger' than yourself – perhaps a religion

Believing in equal rights and justice for all, regardless of background or other differences

Being aware of, understanding and managing your emotions well

Being able to evaluate a problem from different perspectives

Not 'showing off' or boasting

Being able to wait calmly and not expecting things immediately

Being methodical and thorough – having the right things and knowing what is coming up

Being yourself, not just copying others but doing what is important to you

Appendix B

STRENGTHS AND DEFINITIONS LIST

Adaptability	Being flexible and able to adjust to different circumstances
Authenticity	Being yourself, not just copying others but doing what is important to you
Creativity	Being original and finding new ways of doing things
Critical thinking	Being able to evaluate a problem from different perspectives
Curiosity	Being interested in new things and asking questions
Emotional intelligence	Being aware of, understanding and managing your emotions well
Enthusiasm	Doing things with energy, eagerness and passion
Equality	Believing in equal rights and justice for all, regardless of background or other differences
Fairness	Giving everybody an equal chance, regardless of your personal opinions
Forgiveness	Excusing people when they have made a mistake and giving them a second chance
Generosity	Sharing your time, belongings or effort with others
Gratitude	Being thankful for good things in your life and positive things that happen
Honesty	Telling the truth
Humour	Being able to see the funny side of things
Independence	Being able to do things by yourself
Kindness	Doing nice things for other people, caring and looking out for others

Leadership	Directing and organising tasks or events and encouraging others to join in
Love of learning	Enjoying learning new knowledge and finding out new things
Modesty	Not 'showing off' or boasting
Open-mindedness	Respecting and considering other people's opinions and points of view; not jumping to conclusions or prejudices
Optimism	Being hopeful and looking for positive things
Organisation	Being methodical and thorough – having the right things and knowing what is coming up
Patience	Being able to wait calmly and not expecting things immediately
Perseverance	Keeping on trying even though things may be difficult or you face setbacks
Reliability	You can be trusted to do what you say you will do
Responsibility	Being trusted to do something and knowing the difference between right and wrong
Self-control	Controlling your thinking and behaviour when it is necessary
Sociability	Getting on well with others in social situations
Spirituality	Believing in something 'bigger' than yourself – perhaps a religion
Teamwork	Working well within a group of people

Appendix C

HAPPINESS SURVEY

Ask the other student and adults in your class this survey. Ask each person to identify their top three answers. There are empty spaces for you to add any answers that are not already on the list.

What makes you happy? Choose your top three answers.

Good health	
Being with family	
Being with friends	
Being by myself	
Doing my hobbies	
Doing well at school	
Achieving my goals	
Dealing with worries	
Being outside	
Being with animals	
Doing exercise	
Getting enough sleep	
Being kind to others	
Noticing the little things	
Being creative	
Looking forward to the future	
Remembering happy things in the past	
Learning new things	

Following a familiar routine	
Trying out new things	

Appendix D

HAPPINESS STATEMENTS

Money makes people happy.	Younger people are happier than older people.	Having power makes people happy.
Being famous makes people happy.	Good health brings happiness.	To be happy you need good friends.
Having nice things makes people happy.	It is possible to be poor and happy.	When we are feeling unhappy, it is possible to do things that will make us feel happier.
Feeling happy is more important than having money, belongings and power.	Happiness depends on life circumstances.	Lonely people are unhappy.

Using social media a lot makes people unhappy.

It is selfish to be happy.

Appendix E

OPTIMIST VS. PESSIMIST CARDS

We are going on a school trip to the museum tomorrow.	There is going to be a new menu in the canteen from next week.	We will have a maths test next week.
A new student is joining our group.	I am going on a holiday overseas this summer.	It is going to rain all day.
My cat has been missing since yesterday.	I have lost my favourite bag.	I have read all the books by my favourite author.
I am starting a new school in September.	I am going out for a meal with my family this evening.	

Appendix F

UNHOPEFUL STATEMENTS

I can't do maths.	I don't understand what to do in science.	Break times are boring.
I'm too nervous to present my work in class.	I made a mess of giving a presentation today.	My friends hate me.
My homework is too hard.	I'm no good at swimming.	The teacher doesn't like me.

Appendix G

PLANNING SHEET

What is the event/situation? (Be specific – what, where, when, who?)	
What are the positives? What are you looking forward to? **What do you hope to learn/improve at/do?**	

What could be a problem?	How could you overcome the problem?

What are the next steps you need to take to prepare?
(Be specific – what, when, who to ask for help, resources needed)

After the event:

- What went well?

- Were there any problems?

- How did you overcome these?

- Which strategies would you like to try/adapt next time?

★

Appendix H

OVERCOMING ANXIETIES

The situation:	
The positives. Why I would like to do this. Why I value/appreciate this opportunity:	What I do enjoy about this situation:
What I do not enjoy about this situation: 1. 2. 3.	Possible solutions or coping strategies:

Appendix I

DEALING WITH SETBACKS

The obstacle/setback I am facing is...	
It is important for me to overcome this setback because...	
What it will look like when the problem is solved...	
My strengths and skills are...	
My current thoughts about this problem are...	I could reframe these more positively to...
My options are... 1. 2. 3.	Pros and cons of these are...
The first option I will try is...because...	
I have been successful with similar issues in the past, for example...	
Steps I need to take for this option (be specific – what, how, where, when)... 1. 2. 3. 4. 5.	Resources I will need (resources, people to ask for help, etc.)

Appendix J

FIXED MINDSET OR GROWTH MINDSET CARDS

FIXED MINDSET CARDS

I'm no good at maths.	I can't do science.	I'm brilliant at history.
I give up.	I won't be able to do this.	I don't have a brain for languages.
I'll never be able to ride a bicycle.	I'll never get any better at this. I won't bother trying again.	I got really bad feedback. This obviously isn't for me.

I'll avoid that. I'll only fail anyway.

I'm good at this. I don't need to try hard.

GROWTH MINDSET CARDS

I can get better at this.

I can't do this yet.

I'm still learning how to do this.

I've improved at this.

I've learned from my mistakes.

This could be a challenge.

I'm going to try hard at this.

I can try another way.

It's ok to make mistakes; that's how we learn.

I can keep trying.	I can learn from this experience.	I like a challenge.

Appendix K

VALUES LIST

Examples of values can include:

- Curiosity
- Accomplishment
- Calmness
- Carefulness
- Achievement
- Adventure
- Challenge
- Determination
- Cheerfulness
- Ambition
- Hard work
- Art
- Education
- Awe
- Belonging
- Energy
- Encouragement

- Enjoyment
- Courage
- Creativity
- Environment
- Hopefulness
- Modesty
- Expertise
- Imagination
- Humour
- Nature
- Individuality
- Open-mindedness
- Family
- Fashion
- Fairness
- Integrity
- Patience

- Independence
- Forgiveness
- Friendship
- Kindness
- Knowledge
- Fun
- Generosity
- Freedom
- Logic
- Helpfulness
- Truth
- Making a difference
- Religion
- Volunteering
- Wisdom
- Success

INDEX OF ACTIVITIES

A

Acceptance 71

B

Being bored 164
Best and the worst case scenario, The 98
Building up a strengths vocabulary 55

C

Careers coaching 178
Challenging unhopeful self-talk 102
Class gratitude tree 125
Collecting strengths 68
Create a yearbook 88

D

Dealing with setbacks 142
Developing lower strengths 70

F

False images all around us 160
Famous people and their strengths 57
Fixed mindset or growth mindset? 147
From unhopeful to hopeful 97
Future hopes 100

G

Gardening and the outdoors 163
Get crafty 116
Goal setting 150
Good and the bad of social media, The 162
Gratitude journal 130

H

Happiness re-set buttons 89
Happiness survey, The 85
Happy Memories Wall 84
Helping others 127

I

Identify 'flow' 112
I'm me, you're you 59

K

Keeping a journal 168

L

Learning from mistakes 139
Learning from success 143

M

Making a difference (group) 129
Making a difference (individual) 131
Move over, anxiety! 120
My sensory profile 165

O

Optimistic planning 103
Optimist versus pessimist 95
Our own strengths 61

P

Past achievements 137

R

Reading 166
Relaxing: What works for me? 167

S

Silent happiness debate, The 87
Skills and strengths swap 65
Stop and savour 114
Strength of the week 56
Strengths surveys 69
Superheroes – from problems to challenges! 141
Superhero mindset 149
Superhero strengths 58

T

Three good things 126
Trying out something new 113

U

Using and managing special interests 118
Using digital technologies 161
Using top strengths to develop lower
    strengths 62

W

What are my strengths? 67
What autism means to me 73
What can exercise do for us? 158
What is happiness? 86
What is important to you? Values clarifier
    176
What is resilience? 138
What makes me happy? 89

INDEX

active listening 31–3
alexithymia 21
Aristotle 79
Asperger Syndrome 11, 12, 23
  see also autism
attention 29
  shifting of 111
attention deficit hyperactivity disorder
    (ADHD) 25, 110
autism 10, 12, 16–17, 19–28
  acceptance 52, 71, 75
  awareness 76
  definition 16, 1–0
  diagnosis 23
  difficulties 20–3
  females 24
  friendly environments 36, 171–3
  and gratitude 124–5
  and happiness 8, 78–81
  media portrayals 24
  and mental health 9, 16, 24, 46, 54, 82
  prevalence 19
  and resilience 136
  strengths 52–4, 71
  and wellbeing 45, 154–8
  see also working with autistic students
autism spectrum disorder (ASD) see autism

behaviour
  disruptive 36
  repetitive 21, 24
bibliotherapy see reading
body image 170–1
'broaden and build' theory 77

careers coaching 178–9
character strengths 48–52
  and autism 52–4, 71
  classifications 51
  lesser strengths 62–4, 70

surveys 51, 69
vocabulary of 55–6, 74
communication
  adult 10, 74–6, 91–2, 105–6, 122–3,
    132–3, 144, 151–2, 170–1, 180
  difficulties 20–1, 27
  social 20–1
  see also active listening
comparisons, negative 82, 91, 133
concentration 33–5
crafting 117
Csikszentmihalyi, M. 40, 106–8

disability, models of 25
DSM-5 12, 23
Dweck, C. 144

eating disorders 156
echolalia 20
education system, UK 11
emotions
  expressing 25, 168–9
  negative 77
  positive 77–8
executive functioning 94, 106
exercise 155–6

feelings, mislabelling 30–1
fixed mindset 144–6
Fleming, A. 139
flourishing 80
flow 40, 106–9, 112–3, 122
  and autism 109–10
Fredrickson, B. 77, 80

Gallup StrengthsFinder 51
gifted and talented 49
goal setting 147

gratitude 123–4
  and autism 124–5
  interventions 123
GREAT DREAM 42–3
group agreement 30
growth mindset 144–7

happiness 8, 78–81
  and autism 45, 81–3
  surveys 46, 80
  and wealth 42, 44, 80
healthy eating 156, 170
high functioning autism (HFA) 23
hope 92–4
hopeful self-talk 103, 105

journaling 168–9

kindness 123–4

language
  adult use 152, 170–1
  identity-first 12
  people-first 12
literal thinking 34, 91, 94, 171

masking 24
meaning and purpose 174–5
mental health needs 9, 16, 24, 46, 54, 82
motor skills 23

negativity bias 93–4
neurodiversity 25–6
neurotypical expectations 53, 124

optimism 92–3, 95–6, 106
  and autism 94–5

PDD-NOS 23
pessimism 93, 95–6, 105
positive psychology 7, 10, 17, 40–7
positive reminiscence 85, 91
'positive thinking' 47
problem solving strategies 75
proprioception 23
puberty 157

questions
  leading 33
  open 60

reading 166–7
relaxation strategies 167–8
reset buttons, emotional 78, 89
resilience 134–6
  and autism 136
routine 35, 95

savouring 110–1, 122
school
  difficulties and autism 27–8
  positives and autism 26–7
  system, UK 11
screen addiction 110
self-esteem 16, 53
self-identity 53
self-image 71
Seligman, M. 40, 79–80, 110
sensory differences 21–3, 30, 36, 91, 157,
    165–6
signature strengths 52
Silver, Dr. S. 140
single tasking 111, 122
skills 49, 64, 65–7
sleep 154
'social blindness' 19
social communication and interaction 20
social media 160–3
special interests 21, 24, 109, 118
  strengths 48–54
  see also character strengths
'subjective wellbeing' 80

terminology 12, 76
theory of mind 20, 95, 124
tiredness see sleep

values 175, 180
Vermeulen, P. 46, 83
vestibular system 23
VIA character survey 51, 69

wellbeing 8, 153–4
  and autism 45, 154–8
'wishful thinking' 93
working with autistic students
  adult communication 30–1, 74–6, 91–2,
      105–6, 122–3, 132–3, 144, 151–2,
      170–1, 180
  general approaches 28–30, 33–9
  physical environment 29, 36, 171–3

Victoria Honeybourne is a senior advisory teacher, trainer and writer. Her background is in special educational needs teaching and she is author of a number of books on the topic. She has a particular interest in promoting wellbeing amongst young people and females on the autism spectrum. She has a diagnosis of Asperger Syndrome and lives in Shropshire, UK.